Stealing
Love

Stealing Love

Confessions of a Dognapper

MARY A. FISCHER

Harmony Books

NEW YORK

Copyright © 2006 by Mary A. Fischer
Published in the United States by Harmony Books, an imprint of the Crown
Publishing Group, a division of Random House, Inc., New York.
www.crownpublishing.com

Harmony Books is a registered trademark and the Harmony
Books colophon is a trademark of Random House, Inc.

Library of Congress Cataloging-in-Publication Data
Fischer, Mary A.
Stealing love : a memoir / Mary A. Fischer. — 1st ed.
p.   cm.
1. Fischer, Mary A. 2. Journalists—United States—Biography. 3. Love.
4. Interpersonal relations. I. Title.
CT275.F55587A3 2006
973.092—dc22

2006009437

ISBN-13: 978-0-307-20987-0
ISBN-10: 0-307-20987-3

Printed in the United States of America

Design by Lynne Amft

10 9 8 7 6 5 4 3 2 1

First Edition

*In cherished memory of my mother, Doris June Sayers,
and Charlie and Scout, who taught me how to love*

AUTHOR'S NOTE

This is a true story. Some dates, names, and other identifying details of certain people and dogs included in this memoir have been changed to protect the innocent—and the guilty.

Acknowledgments

I want to thank Laura Yorke, my agent and friend, for passionately supporting the idea when she first heard it and for believing in me—all the way back to the McMartin days. I'm also grateful to Bob Williams, a fellow lone voice in the wilderness, who read every word, twice, and whose integrity and friendship I will always value. Many thanks, too, to Carol Mann; my wonderful editor, Shaye Areheart, who believed in my story; and her associates Josh Poole and Paige Alexander, who helped make it all happen.

For their interest, enduring support, and friendship, I also thank Mary Jane Stevenson, Jonathan Tudor, Tony Ganz, Caren and Oliver Kurlander, Elizabeth Gjelten, Craig Bassett, Kathy Martinez, Cliff Rothman, Kathleen Sharp, Audrey Patrick, Mark MacNamara, Erica Williams, Patti DuPre, Laura Bogner, Sherrie Lea, Juliette Kurth, Jonathan Emerson, Ingrid Young, Jesse Trentadue, Joanne Fischer, Meg Grant, Annie Flower, Mariana Arangua, and Mark and Kim Talbot.

And I thank Diana Beardsley for her many wise insights, and Dan Fischer for his care and clear memories, and for showing me that a different way to be a family is possible.

My deep appreciation also goes to Dr. Janos Kalla, who helped me find my rightful place in the world, and to my partners in crime—you know who you are.

Some of the greatest damage ever done was by people who saw wrong and did nothing.

—MARTIN LUTHER KING, JR.

PROLOGUE

It was late on a November night in 1998 when I made my move. The night air had turned brisk, and a light fog had begun to settle over the street. Traffic had thinned out to one car every few minutes, and people on my block had gone inside for the night. It was eerily quiet except for Sonny's faint, intermittent barking from inside a small shed at my neighbor Hank's house around the corner.

Conditions seemed to be perfect for a clandestine venture. My friend Bonnie, flustered but steadfast, was waiting around the corner in my car, ready to start the engine as soon as I gave the signal. Even the full moon high on the hillside behind my house acted as a willing accomplice, its lunar light so bright and expansive that I would not need to carry a flashlight.

I dressed in black sweatpants, a black turtleneck, and running shoes. I considered wearing a wool knit hat to hide my long red hair, but decided against it, fearing someone might take me for a real burglar and call the police. As an added shield against my identity, I tied my hair up in a green scarf and put on an old pair of eyeglasses.

"Don't do it," my boyfriend, Gary, cautioned, seeing the wild flicker in my eyes. "It's against the law. If you get caught, they could throw you in jail." He was right about that. I could be arrested for trespassing and theft, but by then I didn't care. If anything, I should have taken action months ago when I first saw Hank beat Sonny and kick him in the ribs for trying to escape through the hole in the wire gate. I couldn't get the image of Sonny, isolated and suffering, out of my mind. He was a beautiful yellow-Labrador mix, strong and spirited, and I longed to see him have the happy life he deserved. Clearly this was one of those situations where justice lay on the other side of the law, and besides, I couldn't help it; I was driven by destiny.

Even if neighbors happened to see me, they probably wouldn't put two and two together and assume I was up to trouble, because in everyday life, I always appeared perfectly normal and above suspicion. "Let the authorities handle it," my boyfriend said. "They'll know what to do." Being skeptical of most types of authority, I groaned at his advice. If I had any reservations about my mission, that's all I needed to hear to push me out the door.

Off I went into the still night. As I walked up the street I felt strangely unafraid, emboldened even, convinced that what I was doing was not only right, but also imperative. Dry leaves crackled under my feet as I stepped in front of Hank's fence. All the lights in his house were off. He had left earlier in the evening, but there was no telling when he might return. So I would have to work quickly. I dragged a plastic trash container to the far side of the fence, climbed up on it, then dropped to the ground in his front yard. I tiptoed to the wire gate and unlatched it. My heart raced as I heard a car slow down. Could it be Hank? I was so close, though, only a few yards from the shed, feeling intoxicated by the prospect that if nothing went wrong, I was moments away from freeing

Sonny. Then he, like all the others, could take his rightful place in the world.

If you looked at me, you'd never guess that I'm a thief. I'm a petite, middle-aged woman, a professional journalist, a responsible home-owner, loyal friend and co-captain of my neighborhood watch. During the week, my neighbors see me leave my house for business appointments dressed in tailored suits, pearl earrings, and high heels or loafers, and carrying a briefcase. I'm single, reliable, and I've never—well, almost never—been in trouble with the law.

Most of the time I write about crime and the law for a living, and if I'm known for anything, it's my investigations of miscarriages of justice, heartbreaking stories about innocent people whose lives are ruined when they get caught up in the criminal justice system. My work has earned some awards and given me the reputation of a champion of the underdog, which amuses me because most people don't know just how deep my rescuing impulse goes. With me, as I've said, it's destiny.

But you may be wondering how a respectable, career-driven woman would become involved in such unorthodox missions. The simple answer: I love animals, especially dogs, and I believe mistreating them is inexcusable. And I'm hardly alone. Millions of people share my passion for dogs and appreciate how special and valuable they are. In a world grown harsh and indifferent, they are the incarnation of goodness, life's true innocents that deserve our protection.

However, there is a deeper cause behind my thieving impulse, and like most criminals who would tell you there were mitigating circumstances that led to their illegal acts, I am no different.

I can tell you that I wasn't always so bold and aggressive. I once looked out at the world around me with passivity and indifference. For much of my life, rescuing the innocent, whether people or animals, was the furthest thing from my mind.

The story I have to tell begins more than forty years ago with my own underdog experiences, and I tell it not to elicit sympathy, for I have made peace with the past, but to explain how and why all this got started. It's a story about loss, profound and enduring loss, and the consequences that define my life to this day. What happened all those years ago shaped the person I became, and it's at the root of every story I write and every dog I steal.

Whatever hint of daring I once had was buried under the weight of a succession of losses. One by one, I lost them all: first my mother, then my father, followed by a series of beloved childhood pets, and eventually my sister.

In my case, and that of my mother and sister, loss came in various forms: loss of love, loss of freedom, loss of free will and personal expression, and, for a time, the loss of hope, because we lost so much—each other, our family, our home, and everything that provided and symbolized love and security.

The most dramatic separation—the one that laid the blueprint for the rest of my life, the one that has compelled me finally to write this story—is the one I discounted and buried so that I could survive. One day my mother was there in the kitchen, mixing our beagle Queenie's food to just the right consistency and filling her bowl with fresh water, and the next day she was gone.

It took my mother's death—and an extraordinary criminal case I covered in 1986—for me to wake up and realize that I had this destiny. And that's when my life and career as a journalist began in earnest, as I became irresistibly drawn to the themes of justice and innocence, and to how I could somehow help rectify the wrongs.

I was being interviewed on television in 1990 regarding a story I had written for *Los Angeles* magazine about alleged sexual abuse at the McMartin preschool in Manhattan Beach, California. The media sensationalized the case, which made headlines around the world, and most everyone thought the McMartins were guilty. The press called them "monsters" long before they went on trial, but after investigating the case for several months and meeting the defendants face-to-face in prison, I concluded they were most likely innocent—a view so unpopular at the time that friends and colleagues looked on me as a traitor to common decency. At parties I got into fierce arguments about the case and, in the end, two close friends stopped speaking to me—and still haven't to this day.

The interviewer asked me how I knew the McMartins were innocent. Of course, I didn't actually *know* they were innocent, since I had not been at the school when the alleged molestation took place. But the evidence I had uncovered, combined with a visceral sense of who these people were as human beings, had convinced me that they had been falsely accused.

When I paused to think about my answer, memories and emotions came flooding back as I realized that my connection to the case went much deeper. The McMartin story contained the emotional truth of my own story, which had made me sensitive to cases of injustice and receptive to the idea that people in positions of power and authority can sometimes make mistakes.

Like the McMartin family, I knew something about confinement. I knew about isolation and what it meant to lose my freedom, my family, to be sent away against my will, forced to live under the strict rules of strangers. When I became a journalist and visited prisons all around the country to interview people, I felt as if I were home.

I knew what it meant to be seen as odd, as an outsider, to be so alone that my soul ached. And I knew, too, about lost innocence when all of the women in my family were broken apart and sent away to various institutions—my mother to a state mental hospital, my sister and I to a strict convent boarding school.

Only when I made that connection did my life make sense. Only then did I understand my passionate compulsion to defend the innocent. Only then did I realize that I had my own story to tell.

I started my story with the abused dog Sonny, and I'll tell you later what came of my adventure that night and on the other occasions when I moonlighted as a thief. But first allow me to present my case. I think you'll see that my activities, professional and occasionally illegal, result from experiences universal to us all—loss, grief, hope, and love.

So I'll tell you the story now.

I

It began innocently enough, with an ordinary family. All of us sitting next to the Christmas tree, smiling, the picture of normalcy. A young family just starting out. Our first house, small but cozy. Wedding day photos on their dresser. Our baby pictures on the piano. The white china, rimmed in gold filigree, protected behind the buffet's glass doors. The only thing missing is a family dog—and she would show up the following year.

The photo is what's left. It's the proof we once existed as a family, and sometimes I need the proof. When I found it a year ago, buried in a box in my basement, the image startled me at first because I'm not used to thinking of us as a family. We were like fragments, spun off one by one from a centrifuge that didn't stop whirling until there was no center left. A good friend offered a simple reason for why none of us stuck together: There just wasn't any glue.

I rifled through the box, hoping to find others from that time. I found several of my father with my sister and me, but only this one of the four of us, taken in 1954 in our house in San Francisco. So I examine it closely, as if it were a rare and valuable artifact from a lost civilization, looking for clues that might help me understand why, when we seemed to have it all right there, it wasn't enough.

I scrutinize the face of my father, still so young and handsome, looking for any signs that might reveal dissatisfaction, but I don't find any. With his happiest years surfing in Hawaii already behind him, he looks here like a devoted family man, his arms around me and my mother. I know now that it was an awkward, ill-fitting role that he would soon tire of, so I savor his display of affection—evidence, physical evidence you might say, that he actually loved my mother, and for a short time, including that Christmas day, he may have even embraced the idea of being a father.

In those days I worshipped him and worked hard to win his love. I called him Daddy then—and throughout his life—trying to preserve a close father-daughter relationship.

On to my mother, sitting so poised and graceful like the lady she was, dressed in her favorite forest-green knit suit, beaming—and why not? Everything she desired most is here—a husband she deeply loves, two children to nurture and raise, a comfortable home, even the other love, her baby grand piano that she played effortlessly without even looking at the keys. So, from her, I don't really expect to find anything amiss. It's safe to say she had no inkling of how drastically her life, all of our lives, would change in the coming years.

Back then I called her Mommy, but that, too, would change as speaking that name became awkward for me. For a while I wasn't sure what to call her. Who she was then largely remains a mystery to me, and I view her here as a pretty stranger, a fleeting illusion that soon shatters and disappears. Yet even in the brief time my sister and I had her as our mother, she tried to instill in us a sense that we were special and worthy of being loved. She gave us the only real, uncomplicated love we ever knew—and, it occurs to me now, that's why I never stole from her.

When I look at my sister, Kate, the first thing that strikes me is how sweet and pretty she is, so happy and content, so open to life, that I can't understand why my father didn't value her more. She didn't share my devotion for him; instead, she bristled under his domination and withdrew into herself, finding safety in detachment, separated from us as she is here.

As for me, life couldn't have gotten any better. I have the best position, in my father's arms, and were it not for the fact that I'm clearly the only one with an eye toward opening presents, I would have been perfectly content to stay curled in his embrace. My father and I shared a bond from the beginning, and people tell me I was his favorite. I used to think that made me special, and I suppose a part of me still does. My sister would never admit it, but I think she still holds that distinction against me and wants me to keep paying for it. But what she doesn't know is how much I've already paid.

A few months ago I finally got around to framing the photo, and it hangs now with others in the hallway of my house. One picture shows the three of us standing by a tree, my father's arms around Kate and me, the sun filtering through the leaves, making our hair shiny. Another is of me on my first Holy Communion, taken in the parlor of the convent school where Kate and I lived after Mom left. I'm dressed in a white veil and starchy white dress that scratched my neck, and I think my sweet, innocent nature comes through loud and clear. But when Kate first saw the photo, she groaned, rolled her eyes, and swore that my delinquent side had already begun to emerge. But as best I can remember, with all the nuns around on that holy day, anything improper was the furthest thing from my mind—except maybe escaping from the convent, which I admit was my plan at one time.

I suppose the photo of me on my thirty-fifth birthday, holding Kate's dog, Charlie, in my lap, could be used as evidence that I stole him six months later, since my growing attachment for him is obvious.

Since there is no one left, I rely on these photos, along with my sketchy memory, my illegible journal notes, and my intricate dreams, to help me tell this story. And to do it right, to tell it honestly, I must burrow deep into dark places that once threatened to smother my spirit. And as I return there, deep wounds that I thought had healed long ago now rip open again, and I'm back at the beginning.

When friends drop by my house, they sometimes stop in the hallway and survey the photos. I draw their attention to this one of the four of us, as if to say, *See, I once belonged to a family just like you!* Every once in a while a particularly astute visitor, upon seeing the photos with just the three of us, will ask where my mother is in all of them. Then it comes, slowly at first, the wave of sadness I'm usually so good at holding back.

2

My mother used to say that she was a born mother, which I took to mean she had yearned to be one and that nurturing came naturally to her. However, for many years I didn't know whether that was true because she left us when I was still so young. The landscape of my memory from those years is, I regret to say, almost completely barren. Where did the memories go? Has age simply swept them out, like dust from a cluttered house? Or have they, in kind deference to my heart, been erased? The few memories that do remain—sparse, spindly trees left standing in the dense forest of my consciousness—suggest the tenderness that could have been.

I'm three years old and lying in my twin bed, buried under mounds of blankets, sweating and shaking all at the same time. We still live in San Francisco, and I'm as miserable as I can be, having just come down with German measles. Because my father is German, strict and unyielding, I wonder if I got this particularly virulent strain because I am his daughter. And I would have been undoubtedly better off with a milder case had I, drawing on my mother's Celtic ancestry, come down with Irish measles—if there even were such a thing.

In those days the prevailing medical wisdom had it that light could blind a person afflicted with measles, so my mother had drawn all the curtains in my room. Alone in the dark, I scan familiar landmarks: the antique dresser with a crocheted doily on top, a porcelain music box with a graceful, spindly ballet dancer inside, Kate's bed perfectly made and empty, all intensifying my aloneness. She had been moved unwillingly, and with a fair amount of complaining, as I recall, to the living-room couch to ensure her safety from my disease.

My mother quietly enters the room, as she must have done many times during that siege, and places her cool hand on my forehead. I am still burning up. She brings a cold washcloth, folds and drapes it over my forehead. She sits on the edge of my bed and gently strokes stray, moist strands of hair away from my burning cheeks. Her voice is soft and soothing. "You're on the mend now, sweetheart," she reassures me. "The worst is over." Then I feel safe and secure in her presence, but I'm not sure if I'm supposed to do or say something in return for her kindness. Part of me thinks I should try to make her laugh, as I sometimes do; it amuses her when I imitate our next-door neighbor's dog, the feisty Jack Russell terrier, the way he puts his snout straight up in the air, like a snooty aristocrat, to follow some interesting scent. But I'm too weak and can barely move.

A few moments pass, and as she gets up to leave, she kisses my forehead. I try to say, "Don't go, stay a little longer," but my words are too faint and she leaves. It was the first refrain in a lifelong chorus of similar pleas, but as on that long-ago morning, the pleas never got the desired response I was hoping for.

As the door closes behind her, I'm again left alone in my dark tomb, when one of the curtains falls open and a thin sliver of light cuts across the foot of my bed and stays there. It's as if a friend has come to visit, and we lie there together, my new friend and I, content in each other's company, unwavering, neither of us going anywhere, until dusk comes and the light gradually shrinks and disappears.

Many years later, I watched a friend plant a potato in a jar of water, balancing it on the edge with toothpicks. Then she put it on a shelf and forgot about it. Weeks later I noticed the potato again. It had been pushed to the back of the shelf, but what I saw surprised and intrigued me. Despite the lack of care and any direct sunlight, it had not only survived, it had thrived. Its brown nubs, now sprouting green stems, had curled and twisted toward the only available light, which came from a narrow window clear across the room.

That would be my mother's legacy to me—a predisposition to seek out light amid all the darkness. I wasn't to value that inheritance until I was in my thirties, a writer living in New York, feeling lost and alone, and I saw by my mother's example how, from a forgotten place on the shelf, a whole and loving human being could spring forth.

My other memories of her take place the following year, after we had moved to Southern California, where Daddy went into the real estate business. The import-export business he had pursued in San Francisco hadn't worked out, and Mom didn't like him being away so long on buying trips.

According to one story, after I was born, my father went on a business trip to South America and returned when I was two months old. As he stood over my crib, Mom cautioned him not to pick me up. "You're a stranger to her and she might get scared," she said. "Nonsense," he said, reaching into my crib. According to him, I smiled and reached up for his embrace without the slightest hesitation. I cherished his delight in telling that part of the story, and it went into the collection of other evidence I relied on to prove that he loved me.

Kate was born first, in August 1948, into a renewed world of hope after the long, hard winter of World War II. My proud father, playful as usual, wrote to his older brother, Boyce, in Hamilton, Ohio: "Enclosed is a picture of our infant. I urge you to have a gander just so you will both realize you're not the only couple that has produced a high-type breed. I am currently engaged in re-tooling for a male of the same thoroughbred proportions." Two and a half years later he got me instead.

In 1955 we moved to the San Fernando Valley just north of Los Angeles, an area where people from all over the country were flocking. It was like a second coming of the old gold rush, but instead of the lure of gold, the new settlers came for the land. Vast, sunbaked stretches of land that seemed to go on forever. After the war, thousands of acres of ranch land and alfalfa fields were subdivided and sold off to newcomers, and the Valley became the fastest growing area in the country. Tract after tract of mostly plain-looking houses sprang up like weeds, and some streets, including ours, didn't even have sidewalks. Farming gave way to massive airplane plants, and real estate became the booming business to be in.

Daddy was drawn to the speculative frenzy and persuaded Mom to move even though San Francisco suited her refined sensibilities. She was reluctant to leave its gentle, quaint culture for what must have seemed to her an unruly, unsophisticated place. But she loved my father so much that she would have followed him anywhere.

Our life in the Valley seemed idyllic. When my parents bought a nearly new ranch-style house, I thought they must be rich. Who but a well-off family could have a front yard with five trees (one that I climbed), a front porch that ran the length of the house, a circular driveway, carpeting in every room, pine-paneled closets big enough to hide in, and, the ultimate status symbol, a swimming pool in the backyard. We loved our pool and spent much of the spring and summer in it doing cannonballs off the diving board and playing tag.

This is when Queenie, our devilish beagle, entered the picture. It was Mom's idea to get her. I'm not sure who gave her that name, but it suited her perfectly. She wasn't particularly regal, nor was she all that dignified or pretty, but she had an air of entitlement as if she owned the place and could do as she pleased.

Her throne was on top of the lattice that covered the barbecue in the backyard. She used to climb up, seat herself on the beams in front, gaze out over her kingdom, and howl whenever the mood struck her, which was usually at dawn, when we were still asleep.

"Damn dog!" my father shouted one morning. He put on his bathrobe, stormed outside, and dragged Queenie to the garage by her collar, then whacked her several times on her backside with a rolled up newspaper. Mom tried to intervene. "Gordie, stop. Please! She's just being who she is, a dog." It was a reasonable argument, but most of the time, in matters of discipline, my father was immune to reason.

Humbled, Queenie kept to herself for a few days, but then her spirit returned in all its defiant glory and, like a proud warrior back from battle, her pride injured but her will fortified with new re-solve, she climbed back on top of the lattice, taking her position on the front lines, and howled even louder than before.

I loved Queenie almost as much as I loved my parents. She was like a younger, rebellious sister, unafraid to stand up to my father, which is more than I can say for Kate and me. We were sissies compared to Queenie, but we didn't need to defy my father or question his authority; we had Mom there to run interference for us. As she did for Queenie.

I secretly wanted to be like Queenie; I was impressed with her confidence and daring. No one told her what to do, and in that way she was just like Daddy, which is probably why they clashed.

Fortunately for me, Queenie liked to plunge into the pool and show that she was a great swimmer, even though she was on the chubby side, probably because Mom and I gave her so many treats. At first I thought she'd sink like a brick, but whenever she jumped in, with my encouragement, she would paddle doggedly from one side of the pool to the other, her long brown ears floating on the water like velvet wings. When she got tired, I would pull her onto my raft. She was too heavy for me to lift all at once, so I would first grab her front paws then her rump. We would drift together, aimlessly, without a care in the world, and when the raft bumped against one side of the pool, we would head off in another direction.

Most families in the Valley had a house and pool pretty much like ours; I just didn't know it at the time. A new American suburban lifestyle had taken root, and we were its pioneers. Later generations would curse the oppressive urban sprawl, the tacky strip malls, and the horrific traffic congestion that came to define the Valley. Even back then, we hardly walked anywhere. Going from one neighbor's backyard to another for barbecues was about it.

For two good years, until I was four and a half, I was a mostly happy child, born with a sensitive streak that I got from my mother. I was even sensitive about people who said I was "too sensitive." Anything with *too* in it seemed more like a criticism than an observation. I wasn't a very coordinated child and often fell down. Mom was always cleaning off bits of dirt and gravel from my knees before attaching a bandage. My fair skin presented a number of other problems. Only fifteen minutes in the sun left my back and legs streaked with the color of salmon. And I was a prime target for bees and mosquitoes. "That's because you're so sweet" was Mom's explanation, which didn't help ease the itching and stinging pain.

I wasn't crazy about the heat, either. In July and August it got so hot—106 degrees wasn't all that unusual—the air stood still and became so thick it was difficult to breathe. People watered their lawns every day, sometimes twice a day, not that it did much good. By late August the blazing sun had scorched whole sections of grass, turning them into parched brown patches.

Some men walked around bare chested in bathing-suit trunks, and women usually wore shorts and bathing-suit tops that, in some cases like Mrs. Wade across the street and Mrs. Sheller next door, exposed their droopy breasts. At any time of the day or night, you could always see sweat circles under the arms of those people wearing shirts. In our family, Kate and I could go barefoot, except around the pool with its hot pavement. We would laugh whenever Daddy stepped barefoot onto the concrete and hopped around, cursing, as if he were walking on hot coals.

Ordinarily Mom never would have let the neighbors see me in my underwear. She was prudish that way, but in the hottest weeks of the summer, I got to run around without a top, wearing only underpants, always choosing the white ones with the ruffles in back because of the attention adults gave me. "Look how cute she is," they would say. Usually I tended to be shy, but something about wearing those underpants turned me into an extrovert. I would climb the elm tree in our front yard, the one near the street, just so anyone driving by could see my pert, frilly bottom.

People in the Valley used to say you could fry an egg on the sidewalk in the summer, but as far as I knew no one had ever tried it. So Kate and I did. With Queenie standing by, as curious as we were, we cracked an egg on the black, gritty asphalt, since there was no sidewalk. Instead of congealing right away, it spread out in a gooey mess. My sister and I argued about who should clean it up. In my view I had done a service to the neighborhood by proving once and for all that frying eggs in the street was an urban myth, so I shouldn't have to clean up. Kate almost went for it, until the pure baloney of my argument finally dawned on her. "It was your idea, so you clean it up," she said, so I did.

Backyard barbecues were a ritual in the Valley, and one neighbor or another was always hosting one. We would walk in with the standard offerings: bowls of potato salad, hamburger buns, potato chips, and bottles of gin and tonic. When it was our turn to host, Daddy would stand over the grill cooking chicken and hamburgers, and I would stay in the pool as much as possible so I wouldn't have to visit with our neighbors. Even then I liked to observe people, a trait that later proved essential when I became a reporter. I remember thinking that when I grew up, I would never look anything like these adults, never allow my arms and legs to get so flabby or have varicose veins, nor would I get so tanned that my skin looked like brown shoe leather.

And I would never talk about such inane subjects as the weather or the prices one supermarket charged compared to another. Staying in the pool was also my defense against the women who wore perfume to those barbecues. I could never figure out why they did that. We were outdoors, for God's sake, where things were supposed to be natural; but much worse, the sweet fragrance attracted the blood-sucking mosquitoes, which went straight for me.

In our kitchen I liked to sit on the counter, my legs dangling over the side, and watch my mother make piecrust. She was so skillful in kneading the wad of dough and then laying it out perfectly in the pan so the edges lapped over the side without tearing. After she had finished and brushed the flour dust off her hands, we would begin our game. She would pretend to forget that I liked to eat the leftover dough, and she would put the bowl in the sink, her hand gripping the faucet handle. "No, don't!" I would shriek. I needn't have worried; she loved the game as much as I did, but she got her pleasure from knowing that it made me happy.

I have another memory of her in the kitchen. She was chopping vegetables as Queenie stood at her feet, impatient to be fed. Mom stopped chopping, opened a can of dog food, mixed it with dry kibble to just the right consistency, and filled another bowl with fresh water. I was curious about how the dog food tasted, wondering if it was of good-enough quality for Queenie, and I dared my mother to taste it. To my astonishment, she did, then put a small speck on the tip of her finger and offered it to me. "Uggghhh!" I groaned and backed away.

As she put Queenie's bowl on the floor, it struck me that her maternal, caring nature extended to our dog, and that, as with the dough, as with most things she did for me, she had accepted my taste-test challenge because she knew it would make me happy.

I wish I remembered more, but that's all there was, and then she was gone.

3

I never got to say good-bye.

It was the tail end of summer and the elm trees in our front yard looked dead again. The blazing sun had shriveled their leaves, and they looked like sad skeletons on the brink of collapse. In the spring the trees would be full of life again, but inside our house there would be no such renewal in our disintegrating world.

Oblivious to any undercurrents of a coming disaster, my only immediate concern—other than keeping my promise to Mom not to get sunburned again, as I had the summer before—was making it past the den, where my grandmother lay dying, without Kate scaring me.

Kate said later there were plenty of signs of trouble brewing, but she was older than me by nearly three years and remembered more. She remembered Mom crying and pleading with Daddy not to leave her alone as he headed out the door for another night at local bars. And she remembered Mom playing the piano to drown out Daddy's threats of divorce.

Apparently, the trouble began in San Francisco, before the Christmas photo of the four of us was taken, when we all looked so happy. Daddy would say later that Mom changed after they got married and was no longer the fun-loving, glamorous woman he had fallen in love with. She had become possessive and unstable at times, he said, and her incessant talking—her "yammering" is how he put it—was the final straw that drove him out at night. Once, he said, Mom ran down the street after him in her nightgown.

That image still haunts me—a hysterical woman, my mother, in a silk nightgown, running after the man she loves, barefoot, desperate to hang on to him and keep him home.

There are no witnesses to the street scene, so I'm not sure what to make of this piece of evidence. Was her desperate behavior a sign of mental illness? Was it craziness that made her abandon her dignity to pursue love? If so, then I and countless others could be accused of losing our minds in the fevered mania of early love. I can see now how some people might have mistaken some of my lovesick actions for psychosis when it was my turn to fall in love: driving past a lover's house with a wig on; napping in the middle of the day to shorten the time until I would see him again; the obsessive focus on a lover's words, replaying our conversations in my mind again and again, hunting for some undiscovered nugget, real or imagined, that might reflect his true feelings for me.

I used to hold it against Daddy that he stopped loving Mom, because that's when everything started to go wrong. If only he could have been more understanding and tolerant, a devoted family man, faithful and constant like other fathers I met who rolled with the vagaries of marriage, even though some of them looked bored stiff. But then he would have been another man, not my father, and I would not have loved him in the same way.

It's still unclear to me exactly what went wrong between them, but I've surmised that it came down to a clash of basic values. Like most women of her generation, Mom had a simple dream—marry a good man, bear and raise children, and make a comfortable home for them. She grew up in a world inconceivable by today's standards. She was born in Detroit, in 1910, when women were still a decade away from getting the right to vote, and marriage and motherhood were virtually automatic. Women were dependent on their fathers and husbands, incorporated into them like an extra appendage.

My mother accepted her husband's goals and ambitions, his likes and dislikes, his decision to move to Los Angeles. Her place was in the background, in his shadow; his dreams became her dreams. That's what women did in those days, and it undid many of them.

For my mother, divorce was something she never imagined would happen to her. Her parents, Earl and Mary Sayers, were kind, solid people, and they were the model on which she based her expectations. They provided a secure and loving home for her, their only child, and they remained loyal to each other throughout their marriage. My mother grew up a romantic, believing that there was one true love for each person, and once you found it, it would last forever. She believed that the world was a safe place, full of decent people, because that is how it had always been for her.

There was little about Daddy that was conventional. He was a loner with a wild streak, and conformity was not in his nature. It's a wonder, then, that he married at all—not just once, but four times. He rebelled whenever anyone tried to impose rules on him, and in that way, I would eventually be just like him.

Born in 1910 in Covington, Kentucky, he was the youngest of three children. In 1912 his parents moved the family to Hamilton, Ohio, where they opened a successful hardware business. He could have gone into the business, but he bristled under the chafe of Hamilton's small-town values. He sought a larger life, one with adventure, and when he was twenty-two, his older brother, Boyce, drove him to the edge of town and waited until he saw my father get a ride, the first of many as he hitchhiked across the country to California.

If you asked Daddy to do something, like slow down his driving speed or not drink too much, he would press his foot on the gas pedal or order another drink just to show who was boss. He was not the type to punch a clock, nor could he tolerate working for anyone else for very long. A fiercely proud and independent man, he never fit into the constructs of a regimented office job. Nor the day-to-day demands of family life.

He embraced the values and lifestyles of men like Frank Sinatra and Cary Grant, independent playboys who loved the nightlife. For much of his own life, his center of gravity was outside the home, sitting in a classy bar, sipping martinis, smoking cigarettes, and flirting with every good-looking woman who walked by.

Like many women before and after her, Mom was drawn to my father's irresistible combination of good looks, charm, and sense of style. He loved nice things and wasn't afraid to pay the price for them. As a young man in the thirties, when men's shoes sold for two dollars, my father bought a custom-made brown leather pair for twelve dollars, sending shock waves through the otherwise frugal Fischer family.

When they married in 1945, Mom took their "until death do us part" vows seriously, and assumed my father did, too. Still, she might have been able to navigate her way through the disintegration of her marriage had it not been for another traumatic loss—the death of her mother.

I was named after my grandmother Mary Miller Sayers, but I barely knew her. She was already very old when she came to live with us in the spring of 1953 after being diagnosed with stomach cancer. We called her Nanna, and she and Mom were very close, more like best friends than mother and daughter. I knew very little about my other grandparents and rarely saw them. To me they were merely another detached part of our family.

Daddy set Nanna up in the den, our TV room, in a rented hospital bed that had metal sides to keep her from falling out. Mom took care of Nanna until, unable to bear watching her beloved mother slipping ever closer to death, she withdrew into a state of perpetual grief.

Daddy stepped in and took over my grandmother's care, which required a level of patience and fortitude none of us knew he had. Day after day he cleaned her bedpan and gave her sponge baths and never complained about it. When things got really bad, and she lost control of her bowels, he washed off her backside, stripped the bed, and washed the sheets.

Kate and I were forbidden to go into the den, where we would see Nanna shrinking away, the pall of death hovering in the room like smog, but we couldn't help looking in the door every time we passed by on the way to our bedroom. She was usually in the same position, propped up on pillows, looking like a mummy, with only her head and hands outside mounds of blankets. Her skin was paper thin and translucent; her hair, thin and brittle. Kate and I looked at each other in mingled horror and amazement; this was our first encounter with death, and it both haunted and fascinated us.

As the cancer spread and my grandmother's pain worsened, we heard intermittent moaning or sudden, sharp cries of pure agony coming from the den. I made the mistake of telling Kate that the sounds were beginning to frighten me, because then she would wait until I had passed the den, then tiptoe up behind me and shriek in my ear. Naturally, I would scream. Once, Nanna turned her head to see what all the commotion was about.

One day the moaning stopped and two men in uniforms carried

my grandmother, covered by a sheet, out of the house on a gurney. I was relieved in a way. Now, finally, the den would revert back to our TV room, and our lives would return to normal.

But things only got worse. I remember Mom lying on the bed in their room, staring at the ceiling. She couldn't stop crying. To escape her grief, she played the piano, not looking at the keys, gazing straight ahead as if the air just beyond her held some secret or solution to her sadness. She had a favorite tune, "Beautiful Dreamer," and she played it over and over in the weeks after Nanna died. I looked up the lyrics recently and saw how appropriate they were for the way she must have felt at the time:

Beautiful dreamer, wake unto me,
Starlight and dewdrops are waiting for thee;
Sounds of the rude world, heard in the day,
Lull'd by the moonlight have all pass'd away!
Beautiful dreamer, queen of my song,
List while I woo thee with soft melody;
Gone are the cares of life's busy throng,
Beautiful dreamer, awake unto me!
Beautiful dreamer, awake unto me!

Beautiful dreamer, out on the sea
Mermaids are chanting the wild lorelie;
Over the streamlet vapors are borne,
Waiting to fade at the bright coming morn.
Beautiful dreamer, beam on my heart,
E'en as the morn on the streamlet and sea;
Then will all clouds of sorrow depart,
Beautiful dreamer, awake unto me!
Beautiful dreamer, awake unto me!

A few weeks after Nanna died, Daddy took Kate and me next door to the Shellers' house to spend the day. They were nice people with two kids of their own, and we often had barbecues together. We were lucky to have them as neighbors because many times they could have called the police to complain about Queenie's howling, but they never did. They said it was just one of those things.

I don't remember the excuse Daddy gave for why he had to leave us at the Shellers, but I sensed something was up, something important, otherwise why would Mrs. Sheller offer us cookies so early in the day? I sat out by their pool, under an umbrella, as Mom had made me promise that summer, and tried to keep my mind off what was happening at home. Queenie barked a couple of times and I called out to her. She must have been perplexed at being able to hear my voice but not see me.

Overcome by curiosity, I excused myself periodically to use the Shellers' bathroom; it was a ruse so I could look out their living-room window to try to figure out what was going on. On my third trip to the bathroom in twenty minutes, Mrs. Sheller asked if I was feeling all right. I patted my belly to let her think I had an upset stomach, and as I passed by the living-room window, that's when I saw them.

Daddy was guiding Mom by her arm toward his car, and she was crying. Several times she turned toward him with an imploring look. Finally she got in the passenger seat. Daddy pushed the lock down on her door, climbed in the driver's seat, and they drove away.

Through the window I watched the car move slowly down the street and get smaller and smaller, until it reached the corner and then disappeared.

4

The first miscarriage of justice is embedded in my imagination. It happened before a judge in the fall of 1956. That much I know. Daddy provided no other details about the day Mom was officially taken from our lives. "Why do you want to know," he'd say when I pressed him. "It will just upset you." *Why did I want to know?* The same impulse that led me to become a reporter, the desire to get to the bottom of things so I could better understand them.

One day many years later, I was sitting on the hardwood bench in a courtroom in downtown Los Angeles, taking notes on a murder trial for a book I was writing. My mind began to wander, and I imagined that Mom's final moments of freedom happened this way . . .

A hefty bailiff with a gun strapped to his wide black belt brings her out of the side room where she has been waiting in a small holding cell. She is dressed like a criminal defendant in a baggy smock (jumpsuits had not yet been introduced), her hands cuffed behind her back. The deputies don't consider her dangerous, except maybe to herself, but she has tried to wrestle free several times so she can go home and check on her daughters, Kate and me.

As she takes her seat at the counsel table next to my father, she looks around the courtroom for supporters. Perhaps her closest friend from high school, Trudy, or Marshall, her adoring cousin from Kansas. But they are not there. And her daughters, where are they? We are too young and have not been allowed to come. We don't even know this hearing is taking place.

My father, the prosecutor in this scenario, stands before the judge and lays out his case for Mom's commitment to a mental hospital. He speaks of her depression, her bouts of crying, her inconsolable grief after her mother died, her two brief stays at a private sanitarium, and, yes, the time she chased after him down the street in a silk nightgown. He's afraid she will take her own life. She's already tried once, he says. He came home one afternoon and found her in the garage, a cloud of black exhaust covering the car where she sat in the front seat, slumped over the steering wheel.

When he finally told me that story many years later, I didn't know if I should believe him. Was it made-up evidence he used to bolster his case to the judge, to us, to his conscience? Or had she actually tried to kill herself and I was just having a hard time accepting it? Where were her daughters when it happened? Why didn't we know she was so upset? Maybe we could have stopped her. What did the suicide attempt say about her commitment to her children? She still had us to live for, so why did she believe her life was no longer worth living?

As children, Kate and I never knew the truth about why Mom was sent away. We were never sure who was responsible for our sadness, our feelings of aloneness and abandonment, and my interest in the concept of guilt and innocence began back then. We never knew how much of Mom's fate had to do with her sensitive, delicate nature, her sheltered, naive view of the world. Or Daddy's inability to sustain love, his discomfort with displays of emotion, his notion that happiness and love waited outside himself with someone other than the woman he married.

When I began covering criminal trials, trying to figure out which witnesses were telling the truth, a wise lawyer told me that most of the time truth lies somewhere in the middle. Maybe it does, but for a long time I alternated between thinking that my father was completely guilty and my mother was innocent and didn't belong in a mental institution, or my father was innocent and my mother really was crazy. There was no middle ground.

Now I think that reality depends on whom you ask. For example, some friends of my mother wondered if my father got tired of her and simply "put her away." But others who knew our family, and my father and the doctors, said that Mom had a nervous breakdown and could no longer take care of herself. And without money enough to afford a private sanitarium, commitment to a state-run facility was the only option, Daddy said.

I don't know about Kate, but as a child I developed a keen sense of which theory to present when people asked me what happened to my mother so I could maximize the chance to get sympathy and attention. To women I met, I usually hinted that my father was the guilty one, and without fail, they'd look shocked and pat my head or hug me. To men, I shifted gears and made my father the innocent one and blamed my mother's absence on a breakdown. Men didn't always give me affection, but they usually nodded, as if they already had an understanding of these things, believing in the Freudian theories of that day that women could easily become hysterical and go off the deep end.

In the absence of specifics, my own opinion of what happened shifted through the years, although it became easier to blame Mom because she had left me and was not around. To blame Daddy ultimately became unthinkable, as it would hold responsible the one parent I had left and destroy my carefully constructed illusion that he could do not wrong.

In the imagined trial of my mother, no defense of her is presented; none is required. The legal system in those days was stacked against people like her. They had no rights and were subject to "involuntary commitment," the practice that allowed almost anyone to be put away, against his or her will, on the say-so of a family member. The judge pounds down his gavel and signs the court order. My mother stands up to protest, but the bailiff intercedes, takes her arm, and leads her away, crying, her head bowed in shame, out of the courtroom to begin her long sentence.

This part is real. When she was forty-two years old, still in the full bloom of her life, her dreams of family and children shattered, the unthinkable happened. She was committed to Camarillo State Hospital. It was only fifty-five miles north of where we lived, but given how little we saw each other, it might as well have been halfway around the world.

For a long time I honestly believed that the doctors threw away the key and forgot about her, and in a way they did, because she stayed there for the next nine years.

5

A tragic part about all of this is that it probably didn't have to happen. Except for a twist of fate aboard a train, like something right out of a French movie, Mom would have married another man and that, as they say, would have been a whole different story. Another road taken, another cast of characters, a different outcome, and another writer to tell the story because I would not have been born.

In the spring of 1944, my mother kissed her parents good-bye on the railroad platform in Detroit and stepped aboard a Pullman sleeper train bound for New York. She was thirty-four then, not yet an old maid, but getting dangerously close as far as she was concerned. Her single status, however, was about to change. The next day, when the train pulled into Penn Station, she would be meeting her fiancé to discuss plans for their wedding. He worked in insurance and wasn't a particularly exciting man, even by my mother's estimation, but he was stable and reliable, and he adored her.

In the end, wasn't that the most important thing? The man should love you a little more than you love him? That was the advice Mom got from her mother, and many years later she passed it on to me, although neither of us followed it.

For the trip, my mother wore stockings, a suit, and calf leather gloves, and carried her hat. Always a hat. Her mother had instructed her on the importance of being refined and "ladylike," which meant paying careful attention to what she wore. She found her sleeper berth, which was on top, and unpacked her white blouse and black cardigan sweater, clothes that wrinkled easily. In the coach section—her parents had not been able to afford first class— she settled into her seat next to the window. A young man, tanned, with dark wavy hair, started eyeing her. He saw that she was pretty, well dressed, and all by herself.

As steam rose from the tracks and the train jerked out of the station, my mother gazed out the window at the passing office buildings, the industrial smokestacks, the small houses with children playing in front yards, and she thought how well her life was proceeding. From the beginning to now, she had been blessed. Her loving parents doted on her and encouraged her interests in dance and music. At fourteen, she had danced onstage for a Red Cross benefit in New York, and she played the piano so well that churches and schools often recruited her.

Her father, Earl Sayers, was a distinguished-looking man. He wore wire-rimmed glasses and vests with his suits. The family was not wealthy by any means. My grandfather worked in a bank, I believe, but to my mother they stressed the importance of having "class" and associating with people of "good breeding." In her growing-up years, she had many friends and an active social life. Picnics at the beach, in the countryside, horseback riding in the mountains. In photos of her as a young woman, she is always smiling, surrounded by friends or relatives, never alone. Eventually I figured out that her version of happiness derived from something as simple as being close to the people she loved.

After two years of college, she attended a secretarial school and was singled out as the fastest shorthand taker in her class. The distinction would give her an advantage over other applicants when it came to getting a secretarial job, which she planned on doing to augment her future husband's income.

As the train sped past small farms in western Pennsylvania and the powder-blue sky darkened, my mother freshened up, applied a new round of lipstick, straightened her hose, and made her way to the dining car. In those days it was an elegant, special place with fabric-covered chairs, white linen tablecloths, fresh roses in sterling silver vases, and impeccable service provided almost exclusively by black waiters who wore crisp white jackets.

Scanning the room for an available seat, the same young man who had seen her earlier stood up and offered her the seat across from him. She hesitated, wondering if it was proper to accept an invitation from a man she didn't know. He extended his hand and introduced himself: "Hello. I'm Gordon Fischer. I'd be honored if you would have dinner with me."

He had planned it perfectly. A bottle of champagne stood cooling in a silver bucket of ice. He tipped the waiter to take care of them throughout the evening and sat in the less-desirable seat at the table. From her chair, she could glance out the window without her view being partially blocked by the coat closet. He mesmerized her with his perfect manners, his worldliness, his dark maleness, the confident way he ordered their meal.

A diner nearby might have overheard her laugh at his jokes and seen her blush at his compliment that she was the prettiest woman on the train. Gordon would have led the conversation, telling her about his grander side. His two-year stretch in the U.S. Navy's Construction Battalion unit that built bridges and temporary airstrips in

Europe. His happy days in Honolulu, how he surfed "the big ones" at Waikiki Beach, waves that swelled to thirty and forty feet. And he had surfed with the best, men like "Duke"—the world famous Duke Paoa Kahanamoku, Hawaiian world-champion surfer and Hollywood actor who played Polynesians and American Indians—everything except Hawaiians.

During dinner, Gordon pulled out a photo of himself standing in the sand next to his surfboard. He had made the board himself, he proudly told her, out of balsa and koa wood. Big and bulky as a canoe, it towered over him in the photo, but while impressed that he could handle such a heavy board, she was much more interested in him. The photo showed how handsome and manly he was in swim trunks. His body was tanned, trim, and taut, not an ounce of fat.

He told her about the morning of December 7, 1941, when he had witnessed history. From his small cottage near Waikiki Beach, he heard what had sounded like low-flying planes and explosions, and when he ran outside and looked in the sky, he saw hundreds of Japanese dive-bombers, looping back from Pearl Harbor, then out to sea, heading toward Hickham Field.

He told her of his ambitions, and she was again impressed. He was on his way home to Hamilton, Ohio, for a brief visit, but then he wanted to start his own import-export business in San Francisco. He didn't tell her that he had been honorably discharged from the Navy when he developed foot problems, nor did he tell her then the full story about Hawaii, parts that she might not approve of.

He didn't go into how, in 1935, when he was twenty-four, he stowed away on a Honolulu-bound freighter with a buddy, and midway in the Pacific Ocean, the ship's first mate caught them hiding in a lifeboat under the canvas cover. After the boat docked in Honolulu, they were arrested and dragged before the town magistrate. If convicted of stowing away, they would face a year in jail. Their future looked bleak, but fate again intervened in a most unexpected way.

"Please state your name," the prosecutor began.

"Gordon Fischer," he said from the witness stand.

"And where are you from?"

"Hamilton, Ohio."

The prosecutor stopped in his tracks. "Do you know a Boyce Fischer?"

"Yes, sir, that's my brother."

Turns out the prosecutor had known Boyce at the University of Notre Dame in South Bend, Indiana. However, any friendship between them was probably secondary to their having attended the legendary Catholic university. In the end, the prosecutor dropped the charges and helped my father and his buddy find construction jobs in Honolulu.

My father certainly didn't tell my mother, at least not that night on the train, about his marrying a woman in Honolulu and later having the union annulled when he learned that his beautiful wife was a lesbian. (When I grew up, he said his first wife was actually a nymphomaniac, so I was never sure what the real story was.)

None of that would have mattered even if he had told my mother about it. That night on the train, as the flickering lights of small towns sped by like sparkling jewels, I think she fell in love with him and experienced, for the first time in her life, the deep stirrings of sexual and romantic love. I think she believed those feelings would last forever, because months later she broke off her engagement and married my father.

6

Kate and I were asleep when Daddy returned late that night, alone, without Mom. I vaguely remember him leaning over me, and as he kissed my forehead, I smelled his breath mixed with alcohol and tobacco. In the morning at the breakfast table, he explained that Mom was not well and he'd taken her to a hospital to recover.

"When will she be coming home?" I asked.

"Not for a while," he said.

And then everything went blank. I'm sure I cried, but I have no memory of my reaction. It seems odd to me now that I don't remember details about something as important and catastrophic as losing my mother. But I read somewhere that when something is too traumatic to absorb, especially for a child, it goes underground, somewhere deep in the psyche, and plays itself out, over and over again.

Back then I had no concept of leaving or endings, yet it did seem inconceivable to me that a person, especially a mother who was so essential to the family, could be taken away. Just like that. One day she was there and the next day she was gone, with no indication of when she would return. It didn't seem right or fair. What about her children? Shouldn't we have had a say in whether our mother left?

I was aware that something huge had happened and that my world, such as I'd known it, with all its simple pleasures and blissful security, had changed and would never be the same again. A heavy curtain fell when Mom left. My main source of love and protection suddenly wasn't there, and I didn't know what to make of it. Something dark and weighty bore down on me, and reconfigured my foundation; it was no longer solid, and it forever altered who I would become.

The tectonic plates in the deepest part of our beings shifted as we were introduced to a whole new version, a whole other geography, of love, with harsh, unforgiving terrain, challenging but ultimately unattainable mountain peaks and impenetrable borders. Once, we thought of love as being all around us, something that flowed freely just because we existed. But from then on, our experience of it changed, and we subsisted on emotional crumbs because there was nothing else.

Overnight, it seemed, Kate and I slipped into a strange new category of being: motherless children. To our face, the neighbors said things like "Such strong little girls you are. Everything's going to be just fine." Or they'd say, "Don't be sad, girls, you still have your father and each other." When they thought we were outside or in the den, their tone changed. "Poor little things," I'd overhear them saying. "What will become of them now?"

To be a motherless child, especially one whose mother was a mental patient, set us apart, made us unusual, different, and most people usually reacted to us in one of two ways: Adults either smothered us with sympathy, or they, as most kids did, looked away and kept their distance when they saw us, as if we had some disease they might catch.

It would be many years before I realized the full impact that her leaving had on me; all other losses in my life would be filtered through that first one, and I would grieve for so long without there being an ending in sight. Most of the relationships I sought, with women especially, would try to repair the loss as I sought the continuation of my mother's love. No one could ever fulfill such an expectation, and the huge hole left by her absence was never filled.

For a few weeks after Mom left, losing her seemed to have some benefits for Kate and me. Daddy took the position that having been deprived of our mother, we shouldn't be deprived of anything else. Without our even asking, our rations of television and sweets took a big upswing as he allowed us to watch and eat pretty much whatever we wanted. And there was suddenly no shortage of food to choose from. Neighbors dropped by with large pots of soup, cookies, and casseroles, the way people do when someone dies. They always hugged Kate and me and stroked our heads, which made me uncomfortable because I hardly knew some of them.

We got so much attention we didn't know what to do with it. I began hiding in the den behind the couch when I heard a knock at the door. Mrs. Wade, from across the street, was the one exception. Behind her back, kids on the street used to make fun of how big she was, especially her breasts—they were huge, like overgrown eggplants. But now they offered a new source of maternal comfort. When she hugged me at the door, I let my head drop on her chest, in between her warm, fleshy breasts, as I took in her smell of perspiration and sweet talcum powder.

The Shellers were saints. They came by our house nearly every day. Mrs. Sheller washed and dried the dishes when Daddy went to the office, and she took piles of our dirty laundry to her house and returned them in a day or two, all folded in neat stacks. Mr. Sheller helped Daddy clean the pool and move the furniture around in the living room. After Mom left, the first thing to go was her baby grand piano. Daddy sold it to a used-furniture store, and the day the movers came, I watched them unscrew the legs, seal the black shiny lid with tape, and wrap the piano in a padded blanket. They had a hard time maneuvering it out of the house and finally had to take off the front door. That left a big, empty space in the living room, and no matter how much Daddy vacuumed the carpet, he couldn't make the four indentations, where the piano legs had stood, go away.

In private the neighbors discussed Mom and speculated about her condition in hushed tones, the way they did about a scandalous affair. Being sent away to a mental hospital was no small thing. It was almost worse than committing a crime, and it carried a shameful stigma. I don't think Daddy, or even Mom's doctors, knew for sure what her diagnosis was. Those were the dark ages when it came to understanding human thoughts and emotions. At times Daddy said she broke from reality and could no longer function. At other times he said she had lost touch with reality. Most people assumed she had a nervous breakdown, and in the absence of anything more definitive, that's the diagnosis that stuck.

In time, the well-wishers dwindled and we were left alone again to figure out how our new family would work without its center. My father believed the only way to maintain order was through discipline and "running a tight ship." He had been raised that way and knew no other method. His father, William J. Fischer, was a strict, domineering man of German descent who never told his children he loved them. From him my father learned the principle of hard work and that it was "unmanly" to show emotion.

Gone now were the flexible, permissive ways of Mom. There was no such thing anymore as discussing our different points of view. My father's word was final. Gone, too, was the feeling that we were safe. Many years later Kate would tell me that after Mom left, she felt in danger and withdrew into herself, hoping to become invisible as a way to protect herself from Daddy's harsh tirades.

To make things work around the house, he did all the cooking and was pretty good at it. Nothing complicated, well-seasoned fried food mostly: fried ham steak, German fried potatoes, Polish sausage, fried eggs, and panfried steak. My favorite dish was his German pot roast, which he let simmer in a brine of vinegar and bay leaf for three hours until it fell off our forks, it was so tender.

Kate and I had new responsibilities heaped on us. All of a sudden, from the preferred position of being too young to handle much of anything—I was four and a half—I had to take my turn washing and drying the dishes. "But I'm too small," I whined. "I can't even reach the sink." Finally he put a footstool in front of the sink for me.

I hated washing the dishes and employed several ruses to get out of it. When dinner was over and we put the dishes in the sink, I would go to the bathroom and stay there long enough for Kate or Daddy to wash the dishes. It worked a couple of times, but then Kate got wise to me.

"Come out of there, you faker," she yelled outside the bathroom door.

"I'm not faking. I'm really sick."

"You're always sick around this time. Now come out of there."

"I can't. I'm sick to my stomach. Honest."

Kate got most of the responsibility and became an adult long before she was ready. Daddy expected her to step in as a mother substitute and look after me, but she hated the role. She was supposed to make sure I didn't run into the street or fall into the pool. She must have thought that no one was looking out for her, so why should she have to do it for me?

When I started kindergarten later that year, Daddy made Kate take me to and from school on her bike. She hated doing it and thought of me as deadweight, which I suppose I was. She had to stand up and pedal, hard, while I perched on the seat doing nothing. It was especially difficult for her when we crossed Roscoe Boulevard in morning rush-hour traffic, a scary responsibility for a little girl not yet eight years old, and I know she resented me for the burden I had become to her. I tried to hold on to her shoulders so I wouldn't fall off, but she said I dragged her down. So I lightly held on to her waist.

Certain things didn't change. It got very hot that next summer, the elm trees looked dead again, we played in the pool as usual, and Queenie continued to climb on the woodpile or the lattice that covered the backyard barbecue and howl. Only now, out of the blue, she started digging holes under the fence and running away. It worried me. I was afraid a car would hit her, but her escape infuriated Daddy. We went looking for her, sometimes on foot, sometimes in his car. He'd mutter swear words and make threats: "Damn dog. She's going to get it now." She never went very far. We usually found her two blocks away, near an empty lot strewn with bottles and cigarette butts. We spied her white-tipped tail first, pointed straight in the air, her black snout close to the ground, following invisible leads on some tasty scrap of food.

When we got home, Daddy dragged Queenie into the garage

and hit her. I witnessed his brutality, but I didn't try to stop him as Mom had. I just stood there, shamefully mute, believing that was the way it had always been and there was no other way.

I drew closer to Queenie and took more responsibility for her care. I was still too small to handle a can opener, so Daddy fed her, but I filled her bowl with fresh water every day and played tag with her around the pool. I nagged him about the fence until he went out and bought a load of bricks and cinder blocks. We worked on the project together. I handed him a brick at a time to block the sections under the fence most vulnerable to escape and then put back the loose dirt.

As the days passed, I waited and watched with hope and dread, but Queenie never once got out. In the evenings, when it was still light, Daddy let me sit with her outside in the front yard—as long as she was on a leash. I felt proud sitting next to her, showing people who passed by in their cars that I had something of my own, something that belonged to me.

Queenie wasn't the only one who developed bad habits. For my part, I began sucking my thumb and twirling my hair. I twisted a section of hair until it got nice and taut, then snapped it, sometimes tearing a few strands from my scalp. Most people assumed I was just behaving like any nervous child, but Mom would have never approved. "You have such beautiful hair," she used to say. "It's what makes you stand out."

"I don't want to stand out," I would groan. "I want to be like everyone else." But I was set apart with the inevitable nickname Red and the pale white skin and freckles that went along with my red hair.

I kept my other habit secret by sucking my thumb at night, in the privacy of my bedroom, or when I thought no one was watching. Always my right thumb. I tried the left, but it never offered the same satisfaction. Sucking my thumb became as natural and essential as eating food, and the habit nourished me in a primal way.

Then Daddy caught me thumb sucking on the couch. "You don't want to wear braces later on, do you?" he said. "Then you better stop now." His concern about a future problem didn't matter to me. The present moment was all that mattered. And besides, I couldn't stop—not then, not for years.

After Mom left, I clung to my father like a marsupial. Besides love, I was now bound to him by need and fear. The fear that I might lose him, too. In my mind he became a larger-than-life figure and, having no one else, I believed he was everything a man and a father should be. There was little I wouldn't have done for him, and from then on, so I could find ways to be close to him, his interests became my interests.

In the mornings I would sit on the rug near the sofa while he read the newspaper. On the weekends, when he watched football games, I would sit on the floor in front of his chair and root for his favorite team. "Go, Green Bay, go!" I would yell. His first love was the Fighting Irish of Notre Dame. He had gone to college there, playing second string on the football team during legendary coach Knute Rockne's tenure, and it broke my father's heart when his parents, hit hard by the Depression, couldn't afford the tuition anymore and pulled him out after a year. A part of him never got over it. Even in middle age, he remembered the catchy team fight song, which I made a point of learning, and during halftime, to entertain him, I made up a dance cheer as I sang: "Cheer, cheer for old Notre Dame, Wake up the echoes cheering her name, . . ."

I learned the vocabulary and rules of football, such as "break from the line of scrimmage," "fading back," "looking for an opening on the field," "it's first and ten on the thirty yard line." As I got older, I made bets with my father, knowing when to give or get handicap points. Over time, I watched hours of football games and could call various plays before they happened, all of which amused him no end. "So what's it going to be, Mary?" he would ask. I considered the options, whether the field goal kicker would kick a field goal for three points, or the team would continue to scrimmage to make the goal line. When I got it right, which was most of the time, I beamed as I watched my father nod with his approval.

I was court jester to his king, a pawn to his knight. When neighbors came to our house, they'd say, "Where's your little shadow tonight?" When we had a barbecue, I would invent a new role for myself, a kind of nurse to Daddy's surgeon. As he stood over the grill, turning the burgers, I would pass him the spatula, a knife, the salt and pepper. Since he greatly valued his cocktails, I made sure I learned the right way to mix drinks. Gin and tonics were easy: one jigger of gin—Daddy liked two jiggers—then fill the glass with ice and tonic. Vodka gimlets required a bit more care. Too much of Rose's lime juice made the drink too sweet. I played the role of bartender up to the hilt and earned praise from the neighbors. And I pleased my father.

I became his collaborator in pulling pranks on people, in particular Kate. No wonder she liked to find ways to scare me. At my father's direction, I short-sheeted Kate's bed and sometimes strung her underwear over the bathroom mirror. Back then I thought our antics were amusing, but I can see why she thought I was "a brat."

After Mom left, our relationship as sisters was scarred by rivalry. Love and affection had become rationed commodities that we had to work for. We competed for our father's love, until Kate decided not to play the game anymore and withdrew from the ring. I stayed. I willed him to love me. I tried to become just like him, thinking that the more he saw himself in me, the more he would love me. But just the opposite was true.

At times I felt sorry for my father. He was alone with all this responsibility. He felt the loss of Mom, too, but in a different way. Suddenly a man never cut out for family life, a bachelor at heart who didn't know the first thing about raising children, had two girls to raise on his own. "Stuck" is how he described his situation. We wondered if he was joking or really feeling that we were a burden to him.

In those days it was rare for a man to have full-time custody of his children unless his wife had died. I made our novel situation an endless source of curiosity and sympathy, which I milked for all it was worth.

7

In the year after Mom left, Daddy hired a series of housekeepers to look after us, but none of them lasted very long. I remember only one, a cheery, heavy-set woman named Rose who was usually doing something in the kitchen when I came home from school. I would sit at the kitchen table and make small talk while I watched her iron or wash the dishes. Her presence meant I didn't have to do those hated chores, but I liked having her there just so I could be around a woman who was doing things my mother used to do.

Rose urged me to go outside and play with Queenie or the neighbor kids. "It's no fun watching me," she would say, but I just sat there, soaking in her femaleness.

One day I came home from school but couldn't find her. I looked outside, by the trash cans, in Daddy's bedroom, even in the pool, thinking she might have fallen in and drowned. She was nowhere around. Just then Mrs. Sheller came in the house. "Rose is gone, dear," she said. "I don't think she's coming back." I never found out the reason, but I think it had something to do with my father's expectations that she stay longer hours on the nights he took "clients" out to dinner. Even then I suspected he was going out with women, but I didn't want to believe that my father could be done with my mother so quickly, and that he had moved on when I was still sunk deep in sadness.

I often thought about Rose after she left, wondering what the new family she went to work for was like, and whether she liked their children as much as she had seemed to like me. A few weeks after Rose left, I heard Daddy talking on the phone. "What else can I do?" He looked worried, his forehead wrinkled. "It's just not working out. It's not good for them. Not good for any of us. I've called around and this is the best thing."

"Them" was obviously Kate and me, and I figured he was talking about getting a new housekeeper, one who could stay overnight so she'd be there all the time. But he was sinking under the responsibility of raising us on his own, and had found a solution.

"I've given this a lot of thought," he began as we sat down to dinner that night. "This situation isn't good for any of us. I can't work knowing you're home all by yourselves. I worry about you and want what's best for you." I sensed where he was headed and cut him off by asking for more potatoes. He dished some out to me, took a deep breath, and continued: "It's a convent boarding school. Not far from here. You'll live there. But you'll come home for visits. It's for the best. Really."

My mind tried to absorb the shock of being sent away—to a convent, no less—as my heart raced with fear. "What about my Queenie?" I asked.

"I'll take care of her," he said.

It all happened so fast. A few days later he took us to Bullock's department store to buy our school uniforms and other things we would need. I knew my life was about to change again drastically, but like a condemned prisoner allowed to enjoy a final meal, I savored the rare shopping time with my father as we walked past the jewelry counter, the perfume counter, the shoe department. Just like other families.

Now a willing participant in my own banishment, I held the shopping list and checked off the items as we located them: navy-blue uniforms, pleated skirts, white cotton shirts, white socks, white underpants, navy-blue wool jacket, yellow cotton shirtdress, brown saddle shoes. Everything had to carry the brand name on the list, just like in the Navy.

At home, a woman with long brown hair—Daddy's new girlfriend, I think—helped us sew small white labels with our names printed in black on every item, even our socks and white lace mantillas.

In my suitcase I packed a photo of me in a sailor dress sitting next to Queenie, my arm around her, and another photo of Mom, the one of her in a coat and hat, smiling, her left hand on my shoulder. As Daddy loaded our suitcases in the back of his station wagon, I sat on the back porch with Queenie, hugging her. I thought about running away with Queenie but abandoned the idea once I realized I'd probably never find enough food for her. I talked to her, believing full well that she understood me. "Be good," I said. "I'll be back soon."

Ramona Convent was Daddy's salvation, a safe place where nuns would properly raise his daughters. But to me it was a prison where I would serve seven years of loneliness. Back then, Ramona was a Catholic boarding and day school for girls. On the outskirts of Los Angeles, it was run by the Sisters of the Holy Names of Jesus and Mary. The Sisters had come from Oakland in 1889 to start the school at the behest of several prominent San Gabriel Valley families that wanted a good education for their daughters.

As we drove east on the San Bernardino Freeway toward the city of Alhambra, I saw in the distance, poking up through a cluster of tall pine trees, a giant, gleaming gold cross on top of a building's bell tower. "That's it, kids," Daddy said. "We're almost there."

In the front seat sitting next to Daddy, I looped my arm through his and wiggled closer. "Move over, honey," he said. "I can't shift gears with you so close." As we turned into Ramona's driveway, I was struck by all the beauty around us. When Daddy had said we would be living in a convent, I envisioned a cloister of stark, dreary buildings, but this place looked like a sprawling Spanish mission set amid well-tended gardens and groves of elm and eucalyptus trees. On the left we passed Rose Heath, a large grassy area bordered by rows of tall yellow and red rosebushes. Two tennis courts sat in the middle of the black asphalt yard, and off to one side, almost hidden behind a giant eucalyptus tree, was what became the best thing about Ramona—a well-stocked candy store that opened for one hour every day except Sunday. Driving on, we passed a small grotto tucked back from the driveway that would become my private sanctuary. A tall white statue of the Virgin Mary, her gentle, kind eyes cast downward, stood beside a stone bench and a gentle waterfall that trickled into a small fishpond.

My awareness of Ramona's beauty vanished the moment we parked and started up the stairs to the main building and its dormitories. In what would become a chronic condition while I was there, sadness and fear gripped me like a clenched fist in the middle of my chest. We walked into a cavernous, musty-smelling parlor where other girls and their parents were milling around. A large wooden crucifix hung at one end of the parlor; an oil painting of the Virgin Mary, her eyes cast up to heaven, hung at the other.

As I crossed the threshold and stepped onto the dark hardwood floor, I had an eerie feeling that I was being turned over—deposited is how it felt—to a strange, alien world from which I might never escape.

Everything seemed old, and there was a haunted feeling about the place. By the time I got there in 1957, the wood floors and stairs creaked, as did the one elevator outside Mother Superior's office, which usually had an out-of-order sign on it.

In the parlor, I took cover behind Daddy as a slender, towering nun with black-rimmed glasses greeted us. Her name was Sister Agnes Theresa. She oversaw the primary "Infant Jesus" dormitory where the youngest girls—ages six to eight—slept, and though she was cordial on that day with Daddy and the other parents, she was to become the scourge of my life for the next several years.

Back then I didn't think of nuns as fully human. I saw them as part human, part celestial beings. Too remote and stern to be angels, but not completely of this world. For a while I assumed they didn't have the same bodily functions as the rest of us and didn't have to bathe or use the bathroom. They were dressed in black habits with a strange-looking starched, white-mesh headdress jutting out along the sides of their faces that reminded me of horse blinders. It cut off their peripheral vision and often made their cheeks break out in red, blotchy rashes. At first I wondered why they accepted such discomforts, but they soon began to teach us that suffering on this earth was a jump start on the road to heaven.

Sister Agnes Theresa welcomed us by placing her bony hands on Kate's and my shoulders, but we shimmied out from under her grip and clung to Daddy. He motioned for Sister to go with him outside where they could talk privately. I watched from a window as they sat on the stone bench near the fishpond. I didn't need to hear their words to know what they were talking about. Their manners and expressions were serious; neither one cracked a smile the whole time, and I imagined Daddy was telling her about Mom, how she was in a mental institution and would have nothing further to do with raising her children. He had used Mom's situation to garner sympathy with Mother Superior to get a good deal on the tuition— two for the price of one and a half. But Kate and I would pay our own price when we heard the nuns refer to us as "hardship cases."

As I peered out the window, I saw Sister nod her head in understanding, and I knew he had gotten to the part about how difficult it was for a man to raise two girls on his own. If he had ended his story there, Sister might have shown more kindness to me during those early years, instead of becoming a watchful eagle eye with a no-excuses policy. So I knew Daddy had given her the rest of his usual spiel. "No special breaks for my kids. They've got to learn the hard way to be strong. Be tough on them. It's the only way they'll make it. If something happens to me, they'll be on their own."

When they returned to the parlor, I rushed to Daddy and buried my head in his chest, my tears making circles in his shirt. In my desperation, I thought he would change his mind, pick up our suitcases, and take us back home because the whole thing seemed horribly unjust. How could he leave us? He was all we had.

I would have done anything not to be left behind, convinced in the deepest part of me that I would not survive without my father. The rope was being cut and I would drift out to sea, alone, completely unprepared for such a venture. "Please, Daddy," I pleaded. "Don't make me stay here. I'll do all the chores at home from now on." He held me close for a long time, and as he pulled away and started for the door, I saw that he was crying. All three of us cried. We knew in that moment that in some irreversible way our family, however fractured it was, had now broken apart forever.

After Daddy left, Sister took us upstairs in the elevator to our dormitories. With our suitcases, the three of us had to cram into the elevator. It was that small. When Sister pushed the button for the third floor, I let out a gasp. The elevator belched and whined, and I thought that at any moment it would drop to the basement. After that, like most of the other girls, we took the stairs, which thrilled the braver ones as they slid down on the well-polished banisters.

Sister dropped Kate off first at the intermediate dormitory. She turned in the middle of the archway leading into the large room, and we just stared at each other. I wanted to hug her, but I knew that would make her uncomfortable, so I just waved good-bye. Sister put her hand on my shoulder and led me away, down the hall to the primary dormitory. It was just around the corner and only halfway down the hall, but to me it would come to seem like a vast distance because of how seldom Kate and I would see each other.

In the dormitory, I saw twenty small, single beds arranged in four rows, each separated from the next by metal poles with white curtains. Each had its own small dresser and closet. My bed was on an aisle facing two enormous windows that took all of Sister's strength to open even a few inches. Much to my dismay, her bed was at the end of my row, partitioned off with walls and a door.

By dusk most of the other girls had arrived, and in the silence of what was now our new home, we followed the first of Sister's many orders—how our clothes must be arranged. She bellowed that our socks and underwear must go in the top drawer and our sweaters in the second—they should not be hung with our uniforms in the closet.

We changed into our pajamas and knelt on the wood floor beside our beds and prayed, as we would every night. Then we pulled the curtains around us and crawled into our beds. As the sky darkened, a chilly breeze swept through the windows. I was thankful for my small oasis of privacy—my world of one—where I could afford the luxury of crying without being seen. I heard the coughs and muffled voices of the other girls as they tried to adjust to their first night away from home. I wondered if they felt as sad and lost as I did, or whether they had some internal strength that I didn't. I wondered what I had done wrong, what crime I had committed, to make both my parents leave me.

I heard a train passing outside, far in the distance, and the wistful, melancholy whistles deepened my sadness. The train passed every night at the same time and became a familiar sound in my life—something reliable and consistent, like a visiting friend I waited for before falling asleep.

For Kate, everything was different. She didn't mind being at Ramona. She was relieved to be out from under Daddy's domination and happy, I thought, to be free of my pranks and the burden of looking out for her little sister. She could start over with strangers who knew nothing of her past life.

But even with our different feelings about Ramona, we both knew that we were now orphans—orphans of the living—and our survival was now up to us.

8

Mom was in her prison seventy-five miles away, and now I was in mine, confined, cut off from my father and Queenie and forced to follow a litany of rules that far exceeded my worst fears. I never knew there could be so many rules, far more than Daddy's, and it was at Ramona where I eventually learned that unreasonable or just plain ridiculous rules were meant to be broken. In that way an otherwise miserable experience instilled in my life a sense of independent thinking that would come in handy later on.

We had to fold our clothes, even our underpants, in a certain way, flat and square, just like they did in a professional laundry. When we made our beds, there could be no wrinkles in the blanket, and if the corners weren't perfectly square, Sister Agnes Theresa yanked off all the bedding and ordered us to begin again. She must have had eyes in the back of her head because she seemed to catch every violation of her rules.

We walked in single file nearly every place we went, not touching the girl in front of or behind us. There was no talking in line in the washroom, in class, in chapel, or after lights went out. Sometimes we weren't allowed to talk during meals. The nuns intended the silence as prayerful meditation, but sometimes it backfired into uproarious laughter as the cacophony of chewing and slurping sounds, accentuated by an otherwise silent dining room, made us sound like pigs at a trough.

Half of our report cards centered on scholarship, as you would expect, while the other half graded us on social traits and work habits in these categories: Respect at Prayer, Care of Property, Cooperation and Dependability, Personal Appearance, Orderliness, Courtesy and Reverence, and Prompt and Willing Obedience, the latter always proving to be my toughest challenge.

We were graded on our behavior pretty much every waking hour. Our table manners were evaluated by a nun or older student who sat at the head of each table to make sure that, among other things, only our hands up to the wrists rested on the table and that we ate everything on our plates. "Remember the poor, starving children in the rest of the world," the nuns would say. I never questioned that statement until Sister Agnes Theresa directed it specifically at me one evening after I'd been at Romona for a few months. With a disapproving look, she eyed the pile of soggy mush-rooms I'd left on my otherwise empty plate. They were canned, not fresh, and with an oily taste and rubbery texture, as were the oysters. I gagged when I tried to eat them.

Under the spotlight of shame, the illogic of that rule suddenly struck me. How did eating everything on our plates, especially when we were full, correlate with children who were starving? "Wouldn't it be better," I timidly asked Sister, "if we ate less so a portion of our food could be donated to the starving children?" Expecting praise for my brilliant idea (and feeling hope, however faint, that I'd be excused from eating the mushrooms), I was startled when, frowning down at me like an exterminator peering over a minuscule bug, she scolded me for being "insubordinate." I feigned contriteness and ate the mushrooms, gagging at one point to get them down.

In study hall, I looked up her word in a dictionary. *Subordinate* meant "refusing to obey orders or submit to authority." If that's what I had done, in what amounted to my first case of flawless analytical thinking, then it didn't seem all that bad or wrong.

In the beginning, other than that one display of boldness, I was dutiful and timid, just the kind of compliant student the nuns liked. "Look at Mary Alice," they'd say to the other girls. "You don't see her talking out of turn." I didn't like being a model of good behavior, fearing that the other girls would ridicule and ostracize me for being a goody-goody, which I wasn't. Fear, not any moral superiority, produced my mousy behavior, as well as the nearly constant state of misery that left me docile, deflated, and without much oomph, like a flag at half-mast. I felt horribly conspicuous, and at times I thought I was wearing a huge letter *C* on my chest. When word got around about my background, I became known as the girl whose mother was in the crazy house, or "the girl who has a crazy mother." Crazy ranked with death, and few of my fellow students knew how to react to either. When I walked into a classroom or passed certain girls in the hallway, they would look away to avoid any eye contact. Some of the girls ignored me all together.

Once a carefree child, I soon developed the habit of crying. The slightest thing set me off into a dribbling mess. I especially didn't like being called "too sensitive," a description that adults often directed at me. On one Sunday night, after a weekend visit with my father, I was lying in bed sniveling—quietly, I thought—feeling sorry for myself as usual, when I saw Sister's tall dark silhouette outside my curtain. She pulled back the curtain and stood over my bed.

"Mary Alice," she said, "you're a big girl now, and I want you to stop that crying. You'll disturb the other girls."

She didn't threaten to punish me, but she didn't have to. Being exposed throughout the dormitory as a chronic crybaby became my real punishment. I couldn't help it. Feelings of isolation defined my life at the convent. I had very few social interactions, and except for a girl named Carrie, whose mother had died of cancer the previous year, I made no friends at Ramona that I can remember.

Our lives at the convent followed a strict routine with little variation. Mornings began in the same way every day. At 6:30 Sister Agnes Theresa would clank a bell as loud as she could. When I was in a deep sleep, I would sometimes confuse the jarring sound with the fire-drill bell and spring out of bed in a heightened state of anxiety. For the first time in my life, I became anxious about sleeping.

Once we had made our beds, with perfect square corners, of course, we stood at our sinks for a quick wash, then marched single file into the chapel on the second floor for daily Mass. Breakfast, usually oatmeal and toast, followed, and then a bell rang and off we went to our classrooms.

Prayers suffused our lives. Before every meal, before every class, even before gym, and at night, kneeling by our beds, we made the sign of the cross and murmured, "In the Name of the Father, the Son, and the Holy Ghost." For most of my years at Ramona, Catholicism became the new anchor in my life; Jesus Christ and his mother, the Virgin Mary, my surrogate family. During Mass, I would knell in concentrated devotion guided by Father Becker at the altar, but I was even more attentive at the evening Benediction service. It was shorter than a Mass—lasting only twenty-five minutes—which my knees appreciated, since they throbbed and turned black and blue the longer I knelt on the hard wooden bench.

Several times during Benediction I thought I had had a bona fide religious experience (now I think I may have been high on the chapel incense). The combination of certain heart-wrenching hymns we sang, such as "Ave Maria," and the pungently rich and smoky incense that wafted through the chapel went to my head, and I cried, overcome by a sense of longing to come closer to Christ. I thought I was being called to become a nun, and I actually considered it for a while, until I realized I had probably just been lonely and wanted to feel connected to something or someone.

In our free time, the nuns drilled us on social graces and "lady-like" manners. To improve our posture, we walked across the Holy Names family room with a book teetering on our heads. We learned to serve tea, how to converse in a social setting, and how to set a table. "Always serve to your guest's left," Sister would say, "and never, never put the spoon on the inside of the knife." We also learned to embroider and crochet. I liked the idea of making something beautiful with my own hands, yet invariably I dropped stitches without noticing and ended up with a drawer full of botched samples that I could have given only as gifts to someone like my mother, who had appreciated anything I did.

Anything else having to do with "feminine guidance"—the euphemism for things biological like sex and menstrual cycles—we were supposed to learn at home from our mothers. When my classmates spoke about their mothers, I smiled and pretended I was late and had to be someplace else. Off I went to the grotto, where I would often escape to find comfort and privacy. I would sit on the stone bench, the kindly Virgin Mary gazing over my shoulder and protecting me, as I counted the goldfish—there were six—to make sure none had died.

. . .

Back then, in a time much stricter than today, the nuns had complete authority over us. One night, a few months after I had come to Ramona, Sister Agnes Theresa turned out the lights, then suddenly switched them back on. "You are to form a single line and proceed to the washroom immediately," she said. "And there's to be no talking." We put on our robes and slippers and shuffled down the hall, exchanging bewildered looks. We formed two long lines in the washroom, and the whispering began. Lice? But where had it come from? I thought that only animals or people on farms got it, and never at a place like Ramona.

We began scratching our scalps and watching in horror as Sister, using an old pair of black-handled scissors, chopped off each girl's hair in big handfuls as if they were sheep in need of shearing. Mounds of soft blond and brunette hair piled up around our feet. When Sister got to me, my fists wadded up and my neck froze. "Just relax," she said. "It'll all be over in a minute." I had never particularly liked my hair until I saw it curled in piles on the floor.

The unchecked power of the nuns would never be allowed today with all the news stories about clerical abuse, but back then parents freely gave their permission to priests and nuns to discipline their children anyway they saw fit, trusting that they knew best how to raise and educate children. In picking Ramona, Daddy had been impressed with its stated mission: to develop well-rounded young women by means of academic excellence, spiritual depth, moral strength, and personal grace. It sounded good in the school brochure, but the means by which a few of the nuns induced those high-minded attributes was never mentioned. Enforcing discipline and conformity was the first order of business, and individuality was stamped out like a plague.

When a girl did something wrong—in Sister's eyes, anyway—like sneaking food to the dormitory or talking after lights out, she would order us to assemble in front of the dormitory by the windows near my bed, or sit under our assigned sinks in the communal washroom. When we were all present, Sister would drape the frightened girl over her lap, pull down her pajamas or underpants, and smack her several times on her bare bottom. I would cringe, thinking how mortified those poor girls must feel.

For me, nakedness became linked to shame and punishment. Never once did the nuns use the word *vagina*. They said "private parts" or "make sure you wash down there," so I figured there must be something bad or wrong with that part of my body. Until my late twenties, I wore baggy clothes to hide my figure, and I wouldn't let my boyfriend see me naked in the shower or in bed, even when we had sex—not an easy feat when you think about it—because of the shame I felt about my body. Gradually I came around, but it took years of therapy and the patience and understanding of some of my more sensitive boyfriends, who told me over and over again that my body was "beautiful."

The theme of punishment even pervaded our games at Ramona. For a time, my favorite was a sadistic version of Simon Says called Sir Cruely. When it was our turn to be Sir Cruely, we got to order the rest of the girls to do odd, difficult things that carried some element of risk. Like climbing over the chain-link fence, which had sharp barbs on top, in the hope they either couldn't or wouldn't, because then you could inflict a second, more severe punishment on them, and they couldn't fight back. That was the rule. With no power or control in the rest of our lives, Sir Cruely provided us with the rare, twisted opportunity to be in charge.

Only rarely did I get to be Sir Cruely. More often than not I was one of his pathetic subjects, yet it didn't occur to me to step out of line when I was waiting my turn to be punished. It all seemed a normal part of my new life.

The bizarre ritual surrounding bath time wasn't a punishment, but it felt like one. Each week we checked the bulletin board to see which tub we'd been assigned to. All of them were individual tubs enclosed in small, private rooms, but no one wanted the tub that was isolated, off by the seniors' lockers, so the nuns rotated them. Before we could get out of the tub, we had to wait for Sister to come and "check us." That's the phrase the nuns used, and it seemed oddly prurient even then.

When Sister came into my tub room, I stood up reluctantly and moved so slowly she clapped her hands to hurry me along. Standing there completely naked, my spindly, seven-year-old body exposed in front of Sister's piercing eyes, something seemed wrong. She checked my elbows and my neck, and then told me to turn around. That's the part I dreaded the most. There was no dirt on me, so what was she looking for, anyway? I never really knew.

Once I was assigned to the tub off by itself, and what happened there added a new shape to my character. I washed myself according to standard procedure, then waited for Sister to come and check me. Twenty minutes passed, then half an hour. The skin on my fingers and toes began to wrinkle. An hour passed, the bathwater turned cool, and still there was no sign of Sister. I was anxious about what I should do. Get out, dress, and go to my dorm, and possibly risk the consequences of disobedience? Or should I stay, for however long, and follow the rules? I called out a few times, but no one came. I felt sure I was being tested, if not by God, then by Sister. But did I have to prove my goodness at the risk of my skin shrinking?

Then I felt the urge to pee. No bathrooms were nearby, and

even if there were, I couldn't leave the tub room. Sitting in the cool water, its clearness turned murky white by the soap, I felt small and utterly insignificant as it dawned on me that I'd simply been forgotten. I began to cry at the same time the warm, yellow urine swirled up around me. At that moment I reached a crossroads of sorts, as a faint voice buried deep in me spoke up and allowed me to see the first glimmer of my true self.

How could I just sit there like a fool, in a pool of my urine, without a shred of dignity? I got out of the tub at once and began to dry off, unafraid of whatever fate lay in store for me. A few minutes later, Sister rushed in and apologized for forgetting to "check me."

As time passed, I shed more of my passive ways and incurred various punishments as a result. When I was nine, Carrie and I climbed through the hole in the tennis court fence, back through the dense brush that made an ideal hideout. We went there for the sake of adventure, just to explore something new. We were sure no one had seen us, but someone obviously had. The following night, Sister stormed into my tub room carrying a Ping-Pong paddle. She ordered me to get out of the tub and bend over the side. Then, while I was naked, water dripping off my body, my bare bottom staring straight into Sister's angry, contorted face, she smacked me with the paddle several times.

It hurt and I winced, but more than the paddle's sting, I hated being exposed to such a glaring display of unchecked adult power. And I could do nothing about it.

9

For the record, Ramona was—and still is—a respected, well-run school, with many fine teachers who turn out bright and capable young women. When I went back there two years ago to see what feelings it would evoke, I was reminded of how beautiful the grounds are. Rose Heath was still there, as lovely and fragrant as ever, as was my private grotto with the fishpond, although there were no longer any fish in it. And the school was smaller. The Sisters had sold the hilly areas by the pool to a condominium developer, and they no longer took in boarders. It had become just a day school. The building with the dormitories, parlor, and bell tower eventually had to be demolished after the 1987 Whittier earthquake.

As I wandered around the grounds, I saw, too, how my father would have thought it was "the best thing" for us. My memories of the school were filtered through my sad-sack internal state, and a few teachers who had a mean streak. If they are still alive after all these years and I happen to run into them, I wouldn't exactly thank them for the way they treated me and other girls. But at least I'd say hello because, unintentionally, they taught me important lessons about self-esteem.

My third-grade teacher, Sister Sarah Marie, was like Sister Agnes Theresa, both serious and humorless in temperament, but she was built low to the ground, short and round, like a fireplug. She had a perpetual frown, and never once did I see her smile. In class we could never be certain if she was mad at one of us or just showing her normal dour expression.

Even more than learning our lessons, she stressed the importance of obedience and discipline. "They are the building blocks of your character," she reminded us regularly. Since I was a child who knew little of the world, "character" was still a vague thing to me. But I figured she must know what she was talking about, and I tried my best to toe the line.

Periodically, Sister called on a student to recite the multiplication tables or some passage we had read earlier. If the girl fumbled the words and appeared confused, Sister had her start over, coaxing, giving her hints now and again, until she finally got it right. But she wasn't nearly as patient with what she perceived as defiance. If a girl came late to class, or talked out of turn without being called on, or whispered to another student, Sister would usually call the girl to the front of the classroom and order her to put her head in a round metal trash can. The poor girl had to stay in that humiliating position for five minutes, sometimes more, depending on Sister's mood that day.

I was frightened by the thought of being punished that way, so I followed Sister's every directive and tried, at all times, to blend in and hide my personality. *If stand out, dear Lord,* I used to pray, *let it be for my penmanship or devotion in chapel.*

It was raining the day it happened. We traipsed into class, water dripping from our raincoats and umbrellas, leaving a wet mess in our wake. Sister admonished us not to spread any more water on the floor and watch how we walked so we wouldn't slip and fall. The

moment she said that, as I rounded the corner to my desk, I slipped
and fell. Sister scowled and motioned for me to get up and keep
going. Halfway down the aisle, I slipped again, nearly landing on
my back, my arms fluttering madly like a bird ready for takeoff. As
I've said, I was a physically uncoordinated child. What's more, I had
flat feet but didn't know it.

Sister must have concluded that I was mocking her, and
she flew into a rage. But why did my slipping and falling upset
her so much? Maybe liability issues. Who knows? "Miss Fischer,"
she bellowed, "come to the front of the classroom—now!" Trem-
bling, on the verge of tears, I shuffled up the aisle toward the blackboard, and on the way, without meaning to, I slipped again.
She looked at me with disgust, as if I were lower than low, and
then positioned the trash can in front of the blackboard. "You know
what to do," she said. As my head descended into the darkness
of the can, my nose brushed against a browning apple core and
sheets of crumpled paper. It could have been much worse, I remember thinking. If this had happened later in the day, the trash can
would have been full of disgusting things like snot-filled Kleenex;
damp, muddy paper towels; and the smelly remains of tuna sandwiches.

Bent over in such a ridiculous position, I could feel my classmates' eyes burning a hole in my backside. But none of them dared
laugh. They knew they could be Sister's next victims.

I thought my punishment was just about over when Sister ordered me to get up and go into the coat closet. Was she kidding?
The closet was small and narrow, not nearly big enough for even a
small child to stand in. What had I done to justify such extreme
punishment? Her face was grim as she slid the door back in its track
and motioned for me to get in. Jammed in with damp coats, ga-
loshes, and umbrellas, it was impossible to get my bearings or move

around. As she closed the door, I squatted down in the pitch-black darkness, feeling desperately alone.

I ached to be free of this school, to go back home and be with my father. I couldn't bear to spend another month here, let alone five more years. Surely I would die first, if not from some punishment, then maybe from suffocation.

In my misery, I finally concluded there must be something wrong with me that warranted such humiliation. Maybe Sister had seen a deep flaw in me, maybe the same one that had persuaded my mother to leave me. Sister's behavior was wrong, beyond the boundary of what was fair and normal. But we had been taught to respect our elders, our parents, God, our teachers—everyone, it seems, except ourselves.

Somehow I would get a message to Daddy, let him know the reality of my life at Ramona. We weren't allowed to make phone calls, and I suspected the nuns read our outgoing mail. But I had devised a secret code with my father. If I wrote about the sun shining all week, he would know that everything was OK. But if, as I did in my letter after that afternoon in the closet, I wrote that the skies were gray and it looked like rain, that was the signal for him to come and rescue me, or at least call the school.

Every day I expected him to come, blow up at Sister (while all the girls watched), and take me home, permanently. But nothing happened. Maybe the letter had gone astray in the mail. "Did you get my letter?" I asked the next time I saw him. He looked at me with a blank expression on his face. Yes, he had received my letter, he said, but had forgotten the code.

A year later, I had occasion to send him another "gray skies" letter, not that it did any good. It was in the first weeks of spring when, sitting in our classrooms, we heard the huge trucks lumber up the driveway, delivering unassembled rides and booths for Ramona's annual fiesta. As if on cue, the gears screamed as drivers grinded them into lower gear to make it up the last incline near the fishpond. The nuns told us not to go in the yard and get in the drivers' way, so when class let out, we perched on the concrete wall, lined up like flocks of beady-eyed birds. We watched intently as the strong men unloaded the precious cargo. On their own, unconnected to the whole, the pieces of wood and metal were dull and uninteresting. The real thrill began the next day, when the men began assembling the pieces, transforming the blacktop into a magical carnival. They locked in the frames of the Ferris wheel seats, put in the red seat cushions, hammered the oversized teacups into metal runners so they wouldn't come apart in all their wild spinning.

Each year there was a guest of honor, and for entertainment, Mother Superior enlisted the McGuire Sisters to sing. There were three sisters, in their twenties then, and they all had dark-brown hair styled in sticky bouffant flips. They wore matching circular skirts, small colorful scarves tied around their necks, and tight sweaters that Daddy said made them look "stacked." Eventually, as I got older, I would consider them corny and old-fashioned, but for the first few years I stood close to the stage to fully absorb the musical experience. I wanted to dance, full out, but I was shy and acutely self-conscious, and only moved my shoulders back and forth.

Daddy usually came on Sunday, around 11:30, just in time to get in line for the barbecued ribs. On Saturdays, I tagged along with Kate as long as she'd allow it. When she ditched me to be with her friends, I wandered around by myself, stopping at booths crowded with people so I could blend in and not appear to be on my own. Invariably I ran into a classmate whose parents invited me to join them. The trick to responding to these invitations was never appearing desperate or needy, otherwise I could never be sure whether they included me out of pity, which I hated and could sense a mile away, or whether they actually welcomed my company. Either way, they were always so generous and paid for my cotton candy and corn on the cob.

When I was ten, the fiesta's guest of honor was one of my idols, Raymond Burr, the star of the TV series *Ironside*. He played a shrewd, gentlemanly consulting detective, confined to a wheelchair after being paralyzed in an assassination attempt when he was San Francisco's chief of detectives. Chief Ironside was as successful a crime fighter as Perry Mason, a previous Burr television role. The program fascinated me and was my first window into the world of criminal justice. It gave an unrealistic but comforting view of the law, its underlying message being that you should never lose hope because truth and justice always win out in the end.

On Saturday that year, I trailed Mr. Burr for much of the afternoon as he went from booth to booth. Everywhere he went, crowds of people flocked around him, asking for his autograph. I didn't want to be so overtly conspicuous about my interest in him and played it cool. When some of the hangers-on dwindled, I casually sidled up next to him, pretending to be engrossed in the game. We smiled at each other but said nothing.

He moved on to the shooting gallery, and again I casually strolled in his direction. My undercover tactics may have been unnecessary, but I believed it essential that I have a cover in case he ignored me, so I could disappear into the crowd without anyone catching on that he had rebuffed me. At the shooting gallery he smiled at me again, put out his hand, and introduced himself, as if I didn't know who he was. I blushed as I shook his hand. Without thinking, I let it spill out. "I love your show," I said, shyly. "When I'm home, I never miss it."

"Well, that's very nice to hear," Mr. Burr said politely. Then he paused. "If you could have anything at the fair, what would it be?" he asked.

His question caught me by surprise, and I fell silent for a moment, quickly running through my options.

"I'd like to win a goldfish." I replied finally. Mr. Burr swiveled around to locate the baseball booth with the large tank of goldfish, and we walked there together, across the yard, parting the crowds as we went. I wasn't used to being in the center of things, and it felt exciting.

Of course, it still remained to be seen if he could win. He would have to throw three straight baseballs into an open oval hole. It looked easier than it was. All morning I'd watched adults throw the balls confidently, only to miss one or two and be deflated in front of their children. The first game Mr. Burr missed twice. He tried again. A crowd of people had gathered around to watch him, and I feared the pressure would interfere with his concentration and he'd lose again. The third time, he won. Everyone clapped.

He was supposed to get only one fish; that was the rule, but somehow he knew that for the sake of the fish, circling alone in the small bowl, two would be better. He winked at the man, tipped him five dollars, and handed me a plastic bag swollen with water and two small goldfish darting around.

I thanked Mr. Burr. "No. Thank you," he said, putting his hand on my shoulder. "You made me a winner." Where did a man get such nice manners? I wondered. And why out of all the girls milling around that day had he selected me? Whatever the reason, the thrill stayed with me for days.

I ran to the intermediate dormitory—where I slept then—and set up the fish in their temporary home, on the corner of my dresser. Unsure of their gender, I named one of them LG, my father's initials, the other one Burr. I gave the fish to my father the next day so he could take them home. We weren't allowed to keep pets at Ramona, so my father said he would take care of them.

During my visits home, I fed the fish once a day, but it never seemed like enough, so I added another pinch or two. At night, lying in my bed, their bowl on my night table, I found comfort in their proximity. I was curious how—or if—they slept, and I would peer into their bowl but could never stay awake long enough to find out the answer.

A few months passed, and somehow I got the idea that I might be able to get away with keeping LG and Burr at Ramona. They were only goldfish, after all. They kept to themselves, never made noise, and wouldn't disrupt Ramona's regimen like a dog or cat would. And since Sister Mary Francis, a warm, kindly nun, one of the nicest at Ramona, was in charge of my dormitory, I figured she might let me keep them.

I brought the fish back with me one Sunday evening, hidden in a jar of water in my suitcase. I planned to put them on my dresser once I pulled the white curtains. When no one was in the wash-room, I took the jar and filled it with more water. Just then, from out of nowhere, it seemed, the eagle eyes of Sister Agnes Theresa, my archnemesis, caught me, and she swooped down on me.

"What do we have here," she asked, knowing full well they were goldfish.

"Please, Sister, let me keep them." I begged. "They won't cause any trouble."

I should have known better. Rules were rules, but I never expected what followed next. She took the jar, then walked down the hall toward the bathrooms as I ran after her. "No, please don't!" I shrieked. "At least put them in the fishpond."

But it was too late. She pushed the handle and flushed the fish down the toilet. In shock, I stood there frozen, unable to speak. My beloved fish were gone, stuck in some dark storm drain or washed out to sea.

I said nothing to Sister at the time; I'd been taught not to talk back, at home and at Ramona, so I kept quiet. Still, I wanted to expose the injustice of Sister's actions and was certain that once my father got my "gray skies" letter, he would intervene and all hell would break loose.

After a week passed and he didn't call me, I saw Sister in the hallway outside my dorm and decided to confront her myself. It was as if someone else's voice was inside me, urging me on, someone confident and grown up, because I held my head up and looked her straight in the eye. Using the vernacular she could relate to, I told her I thought her actions had been "unchristian" and that God would not look kindly on her killing two of his innocent creatures.

I'll never forget the dazed look on her face. My boldness stunned us both, and for a few moments she was speechless. Then, as I expected, she doled out my punishment—I would have to eat two helpings of mushrooms the next time they were served—but somehow I didn't mind. That voice of defiance inside me was there to stay, and it would serve me better in life than my academic education ever could.

When I was in the fifth grade, my father finally remembered our secret code and came to my rescue. My teacher then was Mrs. Langster. She was the best lay teacher at the school and we liked her, except we couldn't figure out why, when she was probably only thirty-five or so, she dressed like an old lady in plain housedresses and antique, "sensible" shoes. Her hips, though, were the one feature about her that no one could ignore. They were "as big as battleships," my father said after he met her. When she stood in front of the class and wrote on the blackboard, with her backside turned to us, her width and breadth distracted us from the work at hand. And yet Mrs. Langster was married. That perplexed me. I was used to my father's taste in women and figured only the good-looking type had a chance to marry. So how could any man want to marry her?

By then, at the age of ten, I was nearsighted and had trouble seeing the blackboard from my desk in the second to the last row. When I told my father about my failing eyesight, he said I should wait and see if it got worse. All of a sudden, it seemed, I couldn't make out the letters that Mrs. Langster wrote on the blackboard. "Shh, no talking," she said when I asked the girl next to me to read the words. "What seems to be the problem back there?"

"I can't see the board," I said.

"What do you mean you can't see the board," she shot back.

"I mean, I can see the board but not the letters."

She scowled and walked down the aisle to assess the board's distance from my desk. As she approached, her left hip bumped the corner of my desk and all of my books spilled onto the floor. Muffled laughter filled the room, and I pressed my lips together to keep from grinning.

"You know why you act this way, don't you?" she said.

I didn't have a clue what she meant. "Act what way, Mrs. Langster?"

"All this trouble, all this commotion," she said, almost sputtering. "It's because . . . it's because you're just like your mother."

I think now that she knew it was a mistake the minute she said it. But, as they say, the cat was out of the bag. I felt a sharp pain in the middle of my chest, and was ready to cry, feeling exposed with all eyes on me. Her words burned in me all week. I wrote my father a letter again, saying the sky was gray and it had begun to rain, and this time he responded. He called the school and listened to my story.

"I want you to be very sure about this," he said. "You're making a serious charge against one of your teachers, and if I discover you've made this up, there will be hell to pay. Do you understand?"

It was the first time my father took a complaint of mine seriously. The first time he stood up for me, and I couldn't have been more proud. He told Mother Superior about the incident, and the next day Mrs. Langster, with great politeness, moved me to a desk in the front row.

I O

We were sitting on the grass, under a magnolia tree, at Camarillo State Hospital, waiting for Mom to come outside, when I saw my first crazy person. It was a warm, bright Sunday afternoon in the late spring of 1957, one of those gloriously perfect days with a flawless, pastel-blue sky that reminded people why they loved living in Southern California.

Mom had been sent away to Camarillo almost a year ago, and this was to be her first visit with us. Daddy had been afraid the reunion would be emotionally wrenching for us all, and perhaps send Mom into a deeper depression. Reports from the doctors did indicate that she had been going through some tough times, especially the first six months after being admitted. She cried much of the time, they said, and sometimes at night in dreams that turned into agonizing nightmares, she called out for Kate and me and had to be tranquilized.

The doctors told Daddy how important it was that she maintain a close relationship with her family—if not with him, because of their marital problems, then at least with her two daughters. It was a key to her recovery, they said.

Had it been any other place, and not Camarillo, people who saw us sitting there in the shade, apples and cookies spread out before us on a plaid blanket, would have thought how nice it was to be having a family picnic in such a beautiful place.

And it was beautiful on the outside, but inside, as I was to learn years later, it was a grim place of untold anguish and suffering, of lives lost in barren wards, patients' memories and personalities nearly wiped out in rooms marked TREATMENTS.

To get to Camarillo, Daddy drove us north on the 101 Freeway, past the honey-and-plum-colored hills. In a state of expectancy and unknowing, Kate and I distracted ourselves by playing one of our favorite road games. We tried to keep count of the horses and cows grazing on the golden shrub, noting that there were more horses than cows, while usually it was the other way around. Some of the animals raised their heads and looked at the humans speeding by in their vehicles, and seeing nothing that interested them, they turned back to grazing.

A few miles past the town of Thousand Oaks, we saw the green highway sign: CAMARILLO STATE HOSPITAL. NEXT RIGHT. My mood darkened as I read into the words an ominous warning that something bad was about to happen. At the hospital's entrance, we drove up a long, winding road that seemed to go on forever, ascending farther and farther away from the outside world, deeper into the bizarre world that had become my mother's life. Halfway up, we saw sun-flooded fields of perfectly groomed rows of lettuce, strawberries, and potatoes, then on past an orchard of lemon and orange trees when the unmistakable odor of manure swept in the car.

"Phew-wee," I said, holding my nose. "What's that?"

Off in the distance we heard the faint mooing of cows and cackling of chickens, making us think we were visiting a farm instead of the largest mental institution west of the Mississippi River. In those days, Camarillo was both. At its peak in the fififties, when my mother was there, seven thousand patients lived in what amounted to a city within a city. It was a bustling industry in those days, with a bakery, a milking barn, a slaughterhouse, even its own morgue. The staff and mentally capable patients tended the fruit and vegetable gardens and the cows, the pigs, and the chickens that were the source of the hospital's food.

When we finally reached the top, Kate and I were surprised at how inviting the place looked. There was no guard at the entrance and everything seemed peaceful. We had imagined patients stumbling around in chains, screaming, tearing their hair out. With its manicured lawns and white cottages with red tile roofs, all with magnificent views of the Santa Monica mountain range, Camarillo easily could have been mistaken for a summer resort for well-to-do people.

That is, until you encountered a would-be guest, as we did, staggering around the grounds, dazed and bewildered. Disheveled, messy hair, his shirt sticking out of his pants, the man seemed about to topple over as he approached us.

"I'm going home today," he said proudly, one word slurring into the next. "They say I'm all well and I can go home. Can you give me a ride?"

"Don't stare," Kate told me. I couldn't help it. He was the first mental patient I'd ever seen, not some made-up fantasy of one, and I wanted to see, up close, the face of mental illness so I could better understand what had happened to Mom. My only frame of reference was the movie classic *The Snake Pit,* in which Olivia de Havilland played the role of a frightened, irrational woman who had been banished to an insane asylum. I must have seen the film half a dozen

times, always fascinated and repelled by images of wailing patients
clawing at barred windows, others dressed in dirty smocks, some
torn to expose their breasts, their hair matted as they wandered,
drugged and aimless, in the day ward. I put my hands over my eyes
when the staff wheeled a bewildered, screaming woman strapped
on a gurney into the room reserved for shock treatments. Or worse,
into the room marked SURGERY where lobotomies were performed.

"Are we going to give him a ride home?" I asked Daddy, believing we might actually do him the favor. I surmised the answer was
no from his disapproving glare, but didn't see the harm as the man
seemed more drunk than anything else. Several times, at barbecues,
or when Daddy came home late, I'd seen him in a similar state—
wobbly, disoriented, not making sense. So I wondered what made
this man crazy and not Daddy. He appeared to be in his forties, like
my father, but he had the manner of a lost child seeking help from
adults. Several times he bowed to us to show that he recognized our
superior status as people who lived on "the outside."

When Daddy guided the man back toward the patient wards,
Kate and I fell silent, our enthusiasm about the impending visit with
Mom subdued by the unsettling prospect of what condition she
would be in. Then, in the distance, coming toward us across the
grass, we saw her, or who we thought was her. But this woman
seemed old and unsteady on her feet, stooped over as she shuffled
along, holding onto the arm of a dark-skinned man in a white uniform. I felt blood draining from my head and goose bumps spring-
ing up on my arms.

Yes, it was Mom. But how could she have aged so much in
about a year? Her red hair, once so thick and shiny, was now dry

and dull with all the natural waves gone. Once attentive and full of life, she now appeared listless and dazed, her movements slow and tentative, her eyes sad and searching. Her face frightened me the most. Webs of ruptured blood vessels crisscrossed her skin, providing a map of the violence she had endured. It would be years before I understood better what had happened to her: She and thousands of other patients had been subjected, against their will, to paralyzing convulsions of electroshock treatments.

Daddy returned just in time to help her down on our blanket. I could tell he was also stunned at the sight of her. Here was the woman he had once felt passionately about, the woman he had made love to countless times, now white and pasty, drained of life, like a corpse.

Mom flung her arms open and pulled us close to her, Kate first, then me. I had longed for this moment, figuring everything would return to normal once I fell into her embrace. Whatever her condition now, it was only temporary, and soon she would return to her once-vibrant self, and we would be a family again.

Kate didn't see it that way. She was crying when she pulled away from Mom's embrace and saw what I couldn't allow myself to see: The mother we had known was gone. This was someone else, someone sad and lost. Someone who could not save us because she could not save herself.

Mom tried her best to make small talk. How grown-up we looked, she said. How pretty my hair was, so long now—not like hers, she lamented, running her fingers through the choppy remnants of her hair. And Kate, such a pretty young lady. And Queenie, how is that little devil? she asked. I felt comfortable talking about Queenie, so I chattered on and on about her latest antics, her new habit of digging holes under the fence and running away, and our many adventures together. Neither Kate nor Daddy seemed to mind my monopolizing the conversation. It took the pressure off them to say something. Mom smiled and seemed genuinely interested in my long-winded report, so I nattered on.

As the sun slipped behind the mountains and we gathered our things to leave, a light breeze scented with sage swept through the air. We promised Mom we'd come back soon, but I don't think she believed us. And that's when she blurted out, "I don't belong here. Really, I don't."

Her words froze in the air. Kate and I looked at each other and rolled our eyes, trying to deflect the moment's awkwardness. The truth is that we didn't believe her. Seeing her so sad and compromised made us lose faith and trust in her, and from then on, she became diminished in our eyes. In our minds, she had become something odd and foreign, and though I didn't realize it at the time, a part of me buried her that day. That day my sister and I began down the long road that would lead us away from her, as we tried to distance ourselves from something we couldn't fully understand, something so sad and painful that rejection seemed the only way out.

"Now, now, Dorrie, it's all right," Daddy said to Mom. "No more tears." She quickly wiped them away, knowing that her husband didn't like emotional displays, and brushed her hands over her dress, as if smoothing out wrinkles would straighten out her life.

"There, all better," she said. "As good as new."

On the way home, we hardly spoke. I was haunted by the image of my mother being led away as we turned our backs, walking away to freedom. It would be years before I considered her feelings about having been committed. In my childhood narcissism, I felt that Kate and I were the only victims, that Mom had abandoned us rather than stick it out through difficult times. We were not important enough to keep her from leaving, and in her wake she left behind two unformed, insecure beings who would have to sort things out on their own.

It didn't occur to me then how devastated she must have felt about losing everything: her husband, her mother, our home, and her children. It must have been horrific for her to lose Kate and me and miss out on our childhood. All our birthdays, Christmas and Easter, the holidays she loved most. She would not be there to teach us about becoming young women, to guide us about boys, to share secrets only mothers and daughters have.

It was what she wanted most, to be a mother, so it must have been unthinkable to lose us. Maybe she didn't have a choice. Maybe she did have a nervous breakdown, or maybe she believed she was having one because my father and the doctors told her she was. Or maybe being institutionalized was preferable to living in the reality of a ruined marriage and broken family, so she simply withdrew from a world that had no use for her.

"When will we go back and see her again?" I asked Daddy.

"We'll see, honey," he said. "We'll see."

But we never went back to Camarillo.

Once a month we were allowed to leave Ramona Convent and go home for weekend visits. Anticipating the Friday afternoons when Daddy would pick us up, I became almost as excited as when I counted the days before Christmas. On Thursday night, I packed my sparkly blue overnight case, which took all of a minute or two because it was so small. I wanted to be completely ready and not waste a minute of precious freedom.

Come Friday afternoon, at 3:30 sharp, I stood with my suitcase on the top landing of the fire escape outside the seniors' dormitory on the fourth floor, waiting for my father. The height made a perfect lookout station of the driveway. But it wasn't very safe. Two of its metal steps were loose, and when the wind blew or there were too many girls up there, the landing swayed, sometimes vigorously, and the joints creaked. Then we would shriek and clutch onto the railings for dear life. Because our lives were devoid of much excitement, we were aching to experience something out of the ordinary, and secretly loved the thrill of impending disaster.

All through my years at Ramona and into my thirties, I occasionally dreamed about the fire escape. I'd be standing on the top

landing when it began to shake, mildly at first, then fiercely. Somehow, though I was holding on tight, I pitched over the railing and
tumbled through the air, my heart pounding, my mind desperately
grasping for split-second solutions, when I woke up just before I hit
the asphalt. The dream's meaning escaped me as a child, but I came
to understand that it was about the precariousness of life, how it can
change and fall away in an instant.

The other girls' mothers usually picked them up. "How come
your father comes and not your mother?" some of my classmates
asked when they had seen him come for Kate and me several
months in a row. At first I wasn't sure how to answer as I fumbled
through a myriad of lies. "My mother doesn't drive," I would say
sometimes, which wasn't really a lie. She certainly knew how to
drive and would have done so if she'd been allowed to leave Camarillo. At other times I would say that my mother was busy at home,
another lame excuse.

As the months passed, I came to see my father's coming to get us
as special instead of something odd. He would take time off from
his important work in the middle of the afternoon to pick us up, not
wait until evening. Here was indisputable evidence that he found
time in his busy life just for Kate and me, proof to all who saw him
leaning on the hood of his car, smoking a cigarette, that he cared
about us.

Plus he wasn't like other fathers, and my classmates sensed that.
He wasn't rich, but he looked like he was. He liked things of quality
and usually wore pressed slacks, a cashmere cardigan sweater or
sports jacket, and suede or leather shoes.

Usually he was pretty prompt. When I saw the hood of his
white station wagon turn up the driveway, I raced down the fire escape, my saddle shoes clumping loudly on the steps. Once, in my

haste, I forgot where the two loose steps were and caught my foot in the open space between them and tripped. I fell flat on my hands and knees as my suitcase tumbled to the bottom of the fire escape. With hardly a beat missed, I stood up, straightened my skirt, tucked in my blouse, and continued my frantic pace toward his car.

On the rare Fridays when Daddy came late, I went through pure hell. I would stand at my post on the landing, my eyes fixed on the driveway as thirty minutes passed, then forty-five, then an hour. Other girls' mothers came and went, and still there was no sign of him. In those agonizing moments, I passed through fear, anger, and sadness as a harrowing play carried on inside my head with the ending as yet unknown. Had he forgotten this was the weekend we could go home? Or worse, would he ever come again? The idea wasn't that far-fetched. It had happened once with Mom, when I never expected it, so maybe it could happen again. Anything was possible now. Like the unstable landing beneath me, I feared he would pull away and my life would collapse under me.

Then I'd see his car, and the anxiety would drain from me as if a high fever had finally broken and I could be calm and cool again.

Weekends at home, at least for me, revolved around maximizing opportunities for a sense of a normal family life. As soon as we pulled into the driveway, I felt my muscles relax as I forgot about my loneliness and longing. It seemed that longing now filled in for love's absence. But once I was home, it was as if I could breathe again, not the shallow breaths of a nervous hummingbird but full, deep, slow breaths. I was safe again.

I pushed open the car door and ran to the backyard as my fantasies at Ramona unfolded. Being with Queenie would provide the stability I needed. "Here, Queenie!" I called. "I'm home! Where are you?" Within seconds she came tearing around the corner, her tail wagging, her mouth drawn back into her trademark, devilish grin. When I thought of her at the convent, I imagined her as a thinner, less rambunctious dog. I'm not sure why. Maybe I figured she'd live longer that way.

She jumped on me with her front paws and licked my face. I bent down and stroked her head and back. Then she ran off and our game officially began. We chased each other around the yard, stopping only to catch our breath now and then. Our favorite ploy was to stand on opposite sides of the pool and pretend to take off in one direction, only to double back and go the other way. She outran and outsmarted me every time. Only once did I actually catch her. She had gone behind the trash cans in back by the garage to lick something off her paw, when I snuck up behind her and grabbed her around the belly. Startled, she let out a sharp howl. We played until, panting and out of breath, we sat together on the back steps, surveying what had become our own world.

At home, I never wanted to do normal kid things for very long. "Go out and play with the Shellers' kids," Daddy would say.

"I don't want to," I said. "I want to be with you." I preferred to stay close to him so I could soak up the safety and comfort I felt in his presence. It didn't matter what he was doing at any particular time—watching football, cleaning the pool, reading the newspaper. I just wanted to be near him. A few times, when Kate was old enough to babysit me, after dinner on Saturday night, Daddy said he had to leave for an hour or so to meet a client. Kate and I knew that meant he was seeing some new woman. I hated to lose what little time I had left with him and tried, unsuccessfully, to stay awake until he got home.

The weekend always went by so fast. We would no sooner unpack, sit down to a few meals together, play with Queenie in the yard, and suddenly it was Sunday—time to return to Ramona. I would wake up those Sundays feeling anxious, realizing that my remaining hours of freedom were few. As afternoon came, the fist grabbed the center of my chest again and I sulked. Daddy called it the "hangdog look."

Throughout the years, the Sunday drive back to Ramona never got any easier for me. My anxiety grew as we passed certain landmarks—the tool and die factory, the "Ramona" apartment building—and I would know we were almost there. The feeling intensified when I saw the gold cross on top of the tower, and as if on cue, I inched closer to Daddy and looped my arm in his.

And so it went until the middle of my first year at Ramona, just after my eighth birthday, when the inconceivable happened. At home one weekend, I followed my usual routine. "Here, Queenie," I called. "I'm home!" But she didn't come running out. "Here, girl! Where are you?" Maybe she was hiding from me, playing a new game. So I played along and began searching for her in all her favorite hideouts. The garage. Behind the woodpile. Maybe she had run away for good, and I'd never be able to find her. My heart pounded. "Here, Queenie!" I called more desperately.

Daddy called to me from the kitchen window. In the house, he said he had some bad news for me. My first fear was that a car had run over Queenie in the street. "Queenie's gone," he said. "I took her to live on a farm. She kept running away, and I got tired of chasing her. You girls aren't here to play with her, and she's not the same dog when you're gone. It's not fair to her. She'll have more room to run and a much better life now. It's for the best. Really."

There was that phrase again. The best for whom? Certainly not me. I saw his mouth moving and heard his words, but my brain couldn't accept what he was saying. Surely he must be joking, kidding around with me as always. My life would be impossible without Queenie. There had to be some way I could get her back.

"Please, please," I begged. "Don't make her stay on a farm. I'll use my allowance to fix the fence so she can't get out."

I was eight years old and still naive, but not stupid. It occurred to me that the so-called farm didn't exist and, burdened by the task of caring for Queenie, Daddy had simply taken her to the pound and had her put to sleep. I looked at him as grimly as I could.

"Promise me you took her to a farm and not the pound."

"I promise," he said.

"Then take me there so I can see her."

"It's too far. And besides," he said, "she'll have a much better life there."

The shock of losing Queenie seeped in slowly. I refused to speak to my father the rest of that weekend. I stayed in my room most of the time, curled on my bed, crying. Through my bedroom window, I saw dead brown leaves fall gracefully into the still waters of the swimming pool. I looked at the woodpile, the barbecue grill, and the water raft, deflated of air now, lying flat on the cement. All symbols of our once-happy life, and for the first time, I felt the deep, raw emotion of loss.

Love is precarious, I was learning, synonymous with pain and endings. The more I loved someone or something, the more certain it would be lost. If I had a lesson to learn, I must accept the reality that feeling an attachment to anything wasn't a wise course to pursue.

All that month I dreamed about Queenie. In one dream I found her by the on-ramp to the freeway and picked her up. In another she had made her way to Ramona, and I found her sniffing the rose-bushes in Rose Heath.

On my next visit home, I remained firm in my resolve to communicate my anger by ignoring my father. I passed through the living room uttering not one word, and in my huff, I nearly missed what was standing by the window. It was a tall birdcage with a blue-and-white parakeet sitting on its perch. In an effort to soothe my feelings, Daddy had gone out and bought a new pet. No matter how pretty the bird was, I was insulted that he would think that trading my beloved dog for a lowly bird was equitable. I still did not speak to my father that weekend and didn't even open the birdcage until just before we were leaving on Sunday. Up close, I saw how beautiful and sweet she was, and I let her jump on my finger. In honor of my dog, I named her Queenie, which proved not to be a good idea.

Our next visit home was Easter. On Sunday morning, I went to check on my new Queenie and fill her tray with new seed. She was lying on her back, her scrawny legs extended straight up in the air.

"Daddy, come quick!" I yelled. "Hurry!"

He rushed into the living room and surveyed the cage as I stood next to him. The prognosis didn't look good, that much I knew. But I held out hope that Queenie was just sick. I ran to my bedroom and prayed. I begged God to resurrect Queenie and bring her back to life, as he had on the first Easter Sunday with his own son, Jesus Christ. If he could raise a human being from the dead, then certainly he had the power to restore life to a small bird.

Daddy came in my room and stroked my head. "I'm sorry, honey," he said, "She's gone." *So much for the power of prayer,* I thought. Daddy theorized that she had probably caught some virus. I said that without another bird for company, she might have died of loneliness. Daddy put Queenie in a shoebox and we dug a hole in the flower beds along the fence. As I stood over the grave and said my final farewell, I thought how strange it was to lose her on, of all days, Easter Sunday.

12

If we had been allowed into Camarillo's patient wards on the day of our visit, which we weren't, we would have seen dank and dreary halls full of dazed men and women wandering aimlessly in a fog, their brains scrambled by the prevalent therapy of that day—electroshock treatments. Mom would later say she received too many of them to count and that she dreaded and feared every one. She always became nauseous, she said, when the orderlies came for her, usually in the mornings before breakfast. She never consented to the treatments—most patients didn't—but that didn't interfere with the frequency of their application. Back then, consent was not required.

If Mom resisted, technicians strapped her to a gurney or in a wheelchair, tied her wrists to the sides with restraints, and wheeled her to the Receiving and Treatment Center, a ghoulish-sounding place that had surgical rooms, a pharmacy, a morgue, and an autopsy room.

I shudder when I think about what happened next. Mom in a treatment room, lying on a table, uncovered except for her hospital gown, as an attendant places a taut piece of rope or plastic in her mouth so she won't bite her tongue or break her teeth. With electrode pads in a metal headband on her temples, a nurse flips a switch and 140 volts of electricity crackle through her temporal lobes like a thunderbolt of lightning. Her whole body writhes in convulsions similar to a grand mal epileptic seizure, which is intentional. Trauma itself was thought to rid patients of their troubles.

Some patients' convulsions were so violent that bones were broken and all but the barest outlines of their memories and personalities were lost. No one knew exactly how electroshock made depression lift, and sometimes it worked and other times it didn't. Science of the brain was in its infancy, and the treatments were hit-or-miss methods that seemed to follow wartime's scorched-earth policy: To kill the enemy, you must destroy everything around it. Doctors couldn't target specific brain receptors like they do today with antidepressant medications.

At Camarillo, my mother's life was reduced to a dismal routine. Each morning after breakfast, on the days she didn't have shock treatment, she performed one menial task or another. She swept her ward, bused dirty dishes in the cafeteria, and made beds other patients didn't or couldn't make. Later, as orderlies came to know and trust her, she worked outside in the fields, picking strawberries and green beans, grateful for the proximity to nature and the sun's warm, renewing light.

Ironically, psychological therapy was in short supply. Rarely did she have private, one-on-one sessions with a psychologist. Once a week she attended group therapy, which from her description sounded like a quintessential madhouse scene. Many patients were not separated out according to their particular problems. Sometimes Mom found herself sitting next to the man who had strangled his wife. At other times, it was the schizophrenic who threatened to kill everyone in the room.

．　．　．

For a long time, I wasn't interested in knowing what my mother's life had been like at Camarillo. Why should I have to listen to her difficult experiences when she had completely turned her back on me? That's how I saw things then. After she left, sadness eventually blended with anger, and I couldn't shake off my icy resentment. As I got older, she painted a grim portrait of Camarillo, and though in my feigned indifference I ignored or discounted much of what she told me, her account seeped involuntarily into my psyche, further laying the foundation for my eventual compulsion to expose cases of injustice.

She tried to tell me that for some of her years there, the care was minimal. With seven thousand patients, the facility was badly over-crowded. Some patients slept in hallways, and there were virtually no private visits with a psychiatrist unless you were disruptive and out of control, and even then, you could only expect a moment of the doctor's time. And then it was quite possible that you'd end up with an injection of Thorazine—the powerful new drug that had begun to flood places like Camarillo.

In many rooms, the floors were bare and cold, my mother said, the flimsy bedclothes inadequate to keep patients warm at night. Hospital technicians occasionally overmedicated patients as a method of control, she said, and while some nurses and techs were kind, others were mean and uncaring. To restrain unruly patients, a few techs hit them, and one applied a chokehold—which strangled one patient to death, a newspaper article would later report. Mom waited for years to tell me the worst of it: the time an orderly tried to rape her as she lay on a gurney recovering from a shock treatment.

To all of it, I'm ashamed to say, I tuned out and offered her no sympathy whatsoever.

· · ·

For years I believed I'd end up like my mother. When her friends first met me, they couldn't get over how much we looked alike. "Like mother, like daughter," they would say. They meant it as a compliment, but I hated every word. Mom and I were a lot alike, and that's what worried me. We both had red, wavy hair and fair, delicate skin that burned easily in the sun; our birthdays were only four days apart; we loved animals—deer were Mom's favorite—and we felt things deeply.

As I got older, I even inherited her droopy left eye and fear of driving around curves and down hills, so with that level of genetic similarity, I figured my fate as a mental patient was preordained. It was just a matter of time.

What made it worse was that Mom would always try to connect us with comments like "We're too sensitive for our own good" or "Our trouble is that we wear our hearts on our sleeves."

My father must have believed I would share my mother's fate because when I cried, he would sometimes say, "Better be careful or you'll end up just like your mother." One day I came home crying because my good friend Maggie had broken off our relationship. It happened during an argument—I don't remember about what—and I really grieved over losing her. Good friends meant the world to me.

"Get hold of yourself," Daddy said. "Stop crying. That's just the kind of thing your mother used to do. Don't rely on people so much. Be more like me. Be independent. I don't need anyone."

Growing up under his direction, my wires got crossed. He believed emotions were signs of weakness, while stoic detachment from the world showed a person's real strength. *If I could just be more like Daddy,* I thought, *and not cry or be so emotional. If only I could stop longing for love and acceptance, his and other people's, then maybe I could escape what seemed to be my destiny of a breakdown and have a chance for happiness.*

To start building a better destiny, I cut off from my mother in every way I could. When the Sisters asked how I was doing without my mother, I would stand up straight, thrust out my chest, and without the slightest feeling of regret or sadness, I would reply that I had no need for a mother and was doing just fine without one. I buried the photo of her in the bottom drawer of my dresser, under my sweaters, and in time I buried her memory so deep that I barely felt anything at all for her.

The first crack in my armor occurred in 1974, when I was a junior at UCLA. On the list of required reading for my political science class was a controversial book, *The Myth of Mental Illness.* It was written by a psychiatrist, Thomas Szasz, who presented a radical but convincing insider's look at the unchecked power of psychiatrists who decided who in society was mentally sick. He went so far as saying there was no such thing as mental "illness"; only the physical body gets sick, and psychiatrists created the mental concept to further their professional gains.

The book fascinated me, and I began to wonder if my mother had been right when, sitting on the grass at Camarillo all those years ago, she had said, "I don't belong here." If that was true, then what did it say about her doctors, about the judge who had committed her, about my father, and about the entire mental health system? Surely they couldn't all have been wrong? The idea was so threatening to me that for many years I tried not to explore it any further.

I could believe that some individual mental health practitioners made mistakes and that my mother was a victim of the times. In the fifties, when she was committed, the mental health profession was still in the dark ages. Every psychological condition—and some medical ones—whether schizophrenia or depression or alcoholism, even senility, got lumped together under the label of *mental illness,* and long-term institutionalization was often seen as the only solution. Especially if you were female. Many women in that era spent time in institutions. When they fell into a dark mood or had trouble coping with failed marriages, lost love, unrealized dreams, with few options outside of marriage, they withdrew from society.

In 1956 my mother entered a scary, unpredictable world whose foundation had been built on the premise that the mentally ill were wild animals that needed to be tamed and broken. In reading more books—*Mad in America* and *Toxic Psychiatry*—I learned that the early history of mental institutions was about bad science and gross mistreatment, some of it so horrific you have to wonder if the doctors themselves were mad.

Up until 1910, the year my mother was born, "lunatics" were kept in dreary, foul-smelling cells as they were watched over and regularly beaten by their asylum keepers. In the pecking order of society's misfits, mental patients ranked below criminals. "Discipline, threats and blows are needed as much as medical treatment," one doctor wrote in 1912. "Truly nothing is more necessary and more effective for the recovery of these people than forcing them to respect and fear intimidation. By this method, the mind, held back by restraint, is induced to give up its arrogance and wild ideas and soon becomes meek and orderly."

No experimental therapy was seen as too bizarre. Hydrotherapy, used in the twenties and thirties, involved strapping an unruly patient into a hammock suspended in a bathtub filled with cold water, where they stayed for hours and even days. The clinician

Hermann Boerhaave wrote that "the greatest remedy for mania is to throw the patient unwarily into the sea and keep him under water as long as he can possibly bear it to recreate the effect of asphyxia."

The iron cage, a scary-looking contraption into which a patient was locked and then lowered into a deep well or pond, was used in another simulated drowning method. The idea, preposterous to the point of stupidity, was that if a patient nearly drowned but then lived, he would be so grateful that he would forget his troubles. "Blistering" and near-starvation diets were also treatments designed to distract patients from their troubles. Mustard powder was rubbed on a patient's shaved scalp, and once blisters formed and infection set it, "the suffering that attends the formation of the pustules is often indescribable," one physician wrote.

In the thirties, some doctors concluded that the mentally ill were unfit to breed any offspring, so they began sterilizing hundreds of female patients without their consent. When Nazi doctors began performing similar experiments on concentration camp victims, the practice drew heated criticism and was abandoned. Camarillo's first lobotomy was performed in 1952, four years before my mother arrived. With a patient only mildly sedated, a doctor twisted an instrument similar to an ice pick into the base of the forehead where the frontal lobes are located, disconnecting nerves that control certain emotions. If you saw the movie *Frances,* starring Jessica Lange as the actress Frances Farmer, you would know how tragic the results could be. In the film, the once spirited, independent Frances undergoes a lobotomy against her will and becomes so flat and distant, so vague and unmovable, that she can no longer feel much of anything, neither sadness or love.

When my mother arrived, Camarillo was in transition away from asylum methods of abuse to ones concentrating on treatment, but the language and practices indicated they still had a long way to go. Patients were referred to as "inmates," and when they were released—if they ever were—administrators took pride in saying they had been "paroled."

There were no such thing as patients' rights back then. Mental hospitals didn't need consent from the patient or a legal guardian to perform any number of devastating treatments—including lobotomies. Nor did doctors, as they do now, have to decide to commit or release someone after an evaluation period of seventy-two hours. Until the midsixties, many patients like my mother were warehoused, drugged, forgotten, and left to languish.

As one year after another passed, rolling into one another like fog, my mother faced the most frightening prospect of all. Worse than the shock treatments, worse than being drugged much of the time, was not knowing if she'd ever get out of that madhouse.

13

When I had been living at the convent for three years, an unusual thing happened one morning. In the intermediate Sacred Heart dormitory, Sister Mary Francis clanked the wake-up bell as usual. As we dressed in silence, we heard a commotion outside as a flurry of nuns whisked down the hall toward the infirmary, the sound of keys jingling in their pockets. We appreciated the nuns' massive key rings because their sound was often our only advance warning that they were in the immediate vicinity. Otherwise, their soft-soled shoes would enable them to sneak up behind us undetected.

Sister left to join the other nuns and, unattended in the dormitory, we whispered wild theories to explain their sense of urgency. Surely the janitor, a sullen, irascible man who'd been under the thumb of the nuns for years, had taken an ax to one of them, one girl said. Just like Lizzie Borden, another called out. Or maybe Sister Sarah Marie had died (could it be true!), and the nuns had just found her body, someone else said. "Bent over with her head in the trash can," I blurted out, surprising myself with the brazenness of my comment. Muffled laughter erupted in the dorm. Since I had

been thoroughly (or nearly so) indoctrinated with a long list of in-
fractions that qualified as sins, it occurred to me that my joke
teetered on the edge of blasphemy, so I peeked out from behind my
curtain to make sure Sister hadn't slipped in the dorm and overheard me. Much to my surprise, speaking my true mind had an unexpected liberating effect, and throughout the day girls rolled their
eyes and smiled at me to show their appreciation for what I'd said.
That made me want to think of other clever things to say.

Later that day we learned the truth about all the commotion.
Carrie had been rousted from her bed and taken to the infirmary to
receive some bad news in private. Her father had died the night before from a sudden heart attack, and we were told to pray for the
poor, departed soul of Mr. Raskin. Most of us were stunned. We had
never known anyone who'd lost a father—maybe a grandparent, or
an aunt or uncle, but never a father. Death, it seemed to us, came
only for the old and infirmed, like my grandmother, but never
someone as important and essential as a father.

With only Daddy left in the picture—and he was an intermittent presence at that—the loss suffered by Carrie made me feel pan-
icky. I was convinced that I could never absorb or survive a loss of
that magnitude. The death of her father—and mine—would leave
a physical wound of some kind. Determined to console Carrie, I
snuck behind a row of lockers and waited for a break in the swarm
of nuns outside the infirmary. I leaned in the door and waved to
Carrie, but she didn't see me. She was staring at the wall with
a blank expression. No wounds as far as I could see, but no tears
either.

I never saw Carrie again. The last thing I heard was that she
had gone to live with an aunt somewhere in Canada. In the weeks
following Mr. Raskin's death, I pressed Sister Mary Francis for an

explanation of Carrie's detached reaction to the tragic news. Putting her arm around my shoulder, she theorized Carrie had probably been in shock, but her father's death would catch up with her some day. "These things usually do," Sister said.

We believed that terrible things came in threes, so when the janitor's wife died a few months later, I was haunted by the possibility that my father would be next. Until then it had never occurred to me that he might die suddenly, though when I thought about it, my face turned ice cold with the stark realization that he was a perfect candidate for sudden death. From all his late-night carousing and drinking, and his smoking (he smoked two packs of Kool cigarettes a day), he had developed high blood pressure and a heart condition. Drinking was as much a part of his life as eating. He drank nearly every night, and when he went out, he had a tendency to drive too fast and take chances on the road. He liked to gun the gas pedal at an intersection when the light turned green and weave in and out of traffic when there wasn't sufficient space as a way, I thought, to demonstrate his prowess and youthful daring.

From that day on, I began to worry that the nuns would deliver bad news to me one morning. Then where would I be without a father? I figured Kate would find her own way without me, perhaps with a friend's family, and I'd be left alone to fend for myself in a world I found increasingly harsh and inhospitable. My destiny seemed clear: If Daddy died or disappeared the way Mom had, I would face a bleak future in which I would be forced, as the expression went, to survive by my wits. I had heard adults use that phrase, but I wasn't entirely sure my mental acumen, as yet undeveloped and underutilized, could supply me with the necessary attributes to survive in the world alone.

My role models became the characters in the novels of Charles Dickens. He wrote about people and circumstances I identified with: society's outcasts, emotional strays, scrappy orphans, outsiders always looking to have their worth recognized and their suffering ended. My hero was Oliver Twist, an enterprising, resourceful orphan who ran away from an abusive workhouse and, to survive, became a pickpocket on the streets of London. Perhaps, like Pip in *Great Expectations,* I'd get lucky and be raised by a secret benefactor.

At night, after final prayers, I would lie in bed and devise various emergency plans in case I lost my father, or some other disaster befell me. I could live with a relative, I thought, maybe my aunt Margot, my father's sister, the prima donna opera singer in New York. But she got on my nerves with all her preening and diva demands, and, in any case, I was fairly certain she wouldn't take me in since, she'd farmed out her only son, my cousin Andre, to military boarding schools. Who else was there? Maybe our former neighbors, the Shellers. Such nice people. I logged that in my mind as a possibility.

Having almost no connection with my mother anymore, she wasn't my first choice, but I included her in my list of options anyway. My brain became a calculator as I ticked off various scenarios right down to precise details. I would sneak into the parlor and use the phone to call her at Camarillo and tell her to come and rescue me. She would have no idea how to get to Alhambra, so I would send her a map. The rest would be up to her, and I prayed she would come up with an ingenious escape plan. The locked wards and bars on the windows at Camarillo would pose a big problem, but patients were always escaping from that place. Orderlies would find them crouched behind bushes in the surrounding hills, in the local bus terminal, and on the main streets of town, trying to hitch rides.

Maybe Mom could escape during the day when patients were allowed to take short walks around the grounds. Where there's a will, there's a way, as Mom used to say.

Failing that plan, I could go to her. I would wear street clothes, instead of my uniform, and keep to backstreets. But that was a riskier scenario because of my age: a nine-year-old, out at night, alone, could attract attention. Still, it wasn't completely out of the question. Stranger things had happened. I would go on like this until, exhausted and overwrought from all my ruminating, I'd finally fall asleep.

Eventually the fear of losing my father seeped into my dreams. They were always the same and would reoccur until I was in my twenties. I would be doing something enjoyable, like swimming or playing on the swings in a park, when in the distance I would see a group of people carrying a coffin into a church. Feeling compelled to follow, I would enter the church and, hoping not to disturb anyone, sit in a pew in the back. When the priest opened the coffin, I would see my father lying there, dressed in a dark suit, his face a chalky white, his hands folded across his chest. Always at that point, I'd wake up, sweating, my heart beating fast.

I felt I had to save my father, find some way to keep him alive; otherwise, with his love also gone, I might not survive. First, I tried flattery and manipulation. When we went out to dinner during our weekend visits, I'd wait until I saw a man around his age who was heavy and out of shape, and I'd say, "You're too smart to ever let that happen to you, Daddy." Or when we were waiting in line at the market and I spotted an obvious human wreck, I'd try another variation: "A handsome man like you would never end up like that." But that approach had no effect, and he would pretty much ignore me.

So I moved on to begging. "Please, slow down," I said when he drove too fast. "You could get in an accident and die." Although I was in the car with him when I said that, somehow it didn't occur to me that my life was worth saving, too.

As I got older, my father developed diabetes. Sometimes I'd come home and find him in the bathroom injecting insulin into his thigh or stomach. The scene scared me, a sobering reminder that I might lose him any day. I would offer my help, but he always closed the door.

Such serious medical conditions required more-sophisticated strategies, so later on when I was living at home I tried bargaining with him. If he wouldn't drink so much, I said, I'd promise to make his coffee every morning and bring in his newspaper. He agreed, and for the next several weeks, as soon as he woke up, I brought him a hot cup of coffee, black like he wanted it, in his favorite gold-rimmed china cup, and the paper, unfolded, with the sports page on top.

As the weeks passed, I saw not an ounce of reduction in his alcohol consumption. Exasperated, I turned to another strategy that became a habit for me, a way of life. I would offer up my life in exchange for his, which seemed so precious and significant compared to mine. At night I prayed that God would take me into heaven before my father. Somehow, it seemed that I could survive my own death. At times I welcomed it, as strange as that sounds.

When I saw that nothing was working, I changed tactics. If I couldn't save his body, I'd try to save his soul. But he was on the outs with the Catholic Church. In catechism class the nuns had told us that if a person died in a state of excommunication from the church, his soul went straight to hell. Many behaviors qualified a person for excommunication. Murder, of course, and other violent crimes, but also far-less-incriminating acts like missing Communion for long periods of time and marrying outside the church. The latter two were Daddy's crimes. There was no official document signed by the pope or someone else high up in the clergy that said he had been ex-communicated, but there was no doubt about it. He had divorced his first wife, the one in Hawaii, and married Mom in a non-Catholic ceremony, then divorced her and remarried twice more, both times outside the church. Moreover, he hadn't received Communion or confessed his sins in I don't know how long.

The thought of my father burning in hell for all eternity, his body engulfed in red-hot flames, was so horrific a prospect I pulled out my ace card. If he would go to confession, receive Communion, and return to the church, I would become a nun. I was fourteen at the time, still under the heavy sway of the church's teaching, and once or twice I had seriously considered becoming a nun. Daddy sat up and paid attention to my offer. I think he figured I'd be safe in a nunnery from the overtures of men like him. He promptly agreed to my terms and returned home one day saying he had just been to confession and Communion. But I didn't think he was telling the truth.

The only strategy left was internal. If I could find a way to be stronger, in my core, to stop crying so much and grow a thicker skin, be more like my father and not need him or anyone so much, maybe I could sharpen my wits as Pip and Oliver Twist did. Then I would be better prepared for whatever life had in store for me.

14

We saw Mom again in February 1959, and this time she came to see us, in our new apartment.

With only Daddy left in our house in the Valley, he had finally sold it the year before, paid off our bill at the convent, and invested the rest of the money in his burgeoning real estate business. "Say good-bye now, kids," he told us one Sunday afternoon as we packed to return to Ramona. "Next time we'll be in a new place."

As I ran in the backyard and surveyed my world for the last time, I saw that it had begun to deteriorate. Some of the beams that supported the lattice sagged, the flower beds where Queenie used to dig were nearly barren, except for a few scraggly rosebushes, and the grass around the pool was now mostly brown patches of dried weeds.

I didn't want to leave our home; it had been my foundation, the vessel through which the spirit of my life flowed, the symbol of our family's brief togetherness, and now it, too, would be gone. Another family would move in, another story would begin.

When I heard my father's voice calling me, I realized that I would be away at Ramona when he packed everything up with the movers. I was afraid he would dig through my belongings and save only those things he deemed essential, so I took his hand and led him into my room. "See this," I said, pointing at my music box. "And this. And these. I want to keep all my books. I know by heart everything that's here, so I'll know if something is missing."

"Don't worry," he said, "I'll pack everything."

"You promise?"

"I promise."

Before everything started disappearing, I would have trusted him and never doubted his word. But now I wasn't so sure. All that next week at Ramona, I couldn't get the fluttering in my chest to stop, a feeling that he would discard something of value to me.

"It's a box," Kate said when we saw our new home, a two-bedroom apartment off Fairfax Avenue right in the center of Los Angeles. It was one of those gaudy stone-and-stucco buildings, functional but uninspired and cheap looking. "There's not even a yard," I said. A small balcony off the living room overlooked the carport and trash cans, but other than that, Kate was right about it being a box. The rooms were small, with brown shag carpeting, ceilings covered in white cottage-cheese plaster, and paper-thin walls.

In the bedroom I shared with Kate, we could hear the man snoring next door at night, another rude awakening. We were now in close quarters with other people. We could see and hear into their lives, as I'm sure they could into ours. It was all he could afford, Daddy said, so we'd better get used to it.

In time we did. The turning point for me came on Christmas morning, three months after we'd moved in. The goldfish incident had happened six months before, in the spring, and when Daddy got impatient with my lingering sorrow, I dared not mention it anymore. Was there something bad or wrong about the length of time I grieved, first over the loss of Queenie, then the goldfish? I didn't want to wallow in sadness, but it was like a river that swelled over the banks with each new loss.

On Christmas morning I was focusing on the presents under the tree when off to my right, in the dining room, I heard chirping. The clear morning light streamed through the window on a bird-cage where a green-and-white parakeet shimmied back and forth on her perch. She was smaller but far more beautiful than her pred-ecessor, Queenie. Her lime-green feathers were accented with iri-descent yellow markings around her neck and chest, making her seem elegant and regal. In choosing a name, with the twice-doomed name of Queenie completely out of the question, and devoid of much imagination, I named her Chirper.

From then on, second only to my father, Chirper became the main anchor in life. When I got home from Ramona and Daddy un-locked the front door, I barged in ahead of Kate and raced to the dining room to make sure Chirper was still in her cage, standing up-right on her perch, alive and well. Then I proceeded with a room-by-room investigation to make sure everything else I valued was still where I had left it and hadn't suddenly disappeared. My blue felt jewelry box, my beaded bracelet, and my toy animal collection—all present and accounted for. I probably could have left the animal toys at the convent, where I had collected many of them during summer camp, but with my trust in the nuns completely gone, I had taken them to our new home, where I thought no one would steal or throw them away.

In February 1959, the Camarillo doctors decided that Mom was well enough to spend the weekend with us. Thoughts of seeing her again put butterflies in my stomach. A lot had changed in the three years since we first saw her at the mental hospital; I had further pulled away from her, disconnecting from the hope that we would live together again as a family.

Kate and I had survived without her, first days, then months, and now years, and there was still no sign on the horizon that she would ever return. I no longer remembered the sound of her voice or what her touch felt like. Her laughter, though, stayed with me, and I smile, all these years later, just thinking about it. It was the kind of natural, unrestrained laughter, especially when she was caught by surprise, that made other people want to laugh, too.

Gone now, I'm not sure where, were my once-vivid fantasies of being rescued by Mom, or when I imagined rescuing her. Gone were my daydreams of our dramatic, tearful reunion, how I'd run into her open arms and stay there until she promised, and I was convinced, that I would never again have to return to the convent and we could finally go home for good.

As we pulled into the driveway that rainy February afternoon, the dark-gray sky made it seem almost like night. Our apartment was on the second floor, and as we walked up the stairs, this time I let Kate and Daddy go in first. There, only fifteen feet from us, was my mother sitting in the rocking chair, her hands gracefully folded in her lap, a big smile on her face. There was my original anchor, in the flesh, not some vague memory or embellished fantasy.

I once yearned to see my mother, but when she stood up and walked toward me with her arms open wide, I took a step back. She looked nothing like I had imagined she would. In my revisionist fantasy, I had replaced the sad image of her at Camarillo with the vibrant, pretty mother of my early childhood.

She wore a kelly-green (her favorite color) shirtwaist dress that enhanced the color of her eyes. Someone had styled her hair and dyed it a deep auburn color. She had used a tawny-colored liquid makeup to cover the broken blood vessels, although she missed a few spots on her face. The powdered rouge on her cheeks had not been fully blended, making her face appear clownlike. In one corner of her mouth, cherry-red lipstick was smeared beyond the outline of her upper lip.

They were the kind of harmless mistakes that women make when they are in a hurry or the light over their mirror isn't bright enough. But under the microscope of our judging eyes, her every word and action were filtered through a harsh and critical lens. At the same time, I wanted to love her deeply again, without reservation, to not feel sorry for her as I did now. I wasn't sure what to call her. Mommy was too intimate, Mother too formal, so I settled on Mom.

When I hugged her and buried my head in her chest, she wrapped her arms around me, and the tension in me let go. "Oh, my two beautiful girls, how I've missed you," she said, tears forming in her eyes. She motioned for Kate to join us, and we huddled in a three-way embrace. I think she wanted to hold on to us forever, but we could accept only a limited show of affection from a woman we hardly knew. So we broke free, and I headed for the dining room, where I knew Chirper would be waiting for me.

When I slid my hand into Chirper's cage, she jumped on my forefinger without hesitation. I gently stroked her back, struck as always by the softness of her feathers. Then, in an effort to ease the tension in the living room, I introduced Chirper to my mother. They exchanged chirping sounds and, without any coaxing from me, Chirper gave her a peck on the mouth and took off, fluttering around the apartment.

Before dinner, Daddy warned Kate and me not to bring up any

topics that might upset Mom, especially anything from the past. So as we sat around the table, we talked about situations and experiences we had never shared together. "Isn't the rain something?" Daddy began. "I wonder when it'll let up?"

"I always liked the rain," Mom said. "Remember that time we . . ." Her words trailed off, and her expression saddened as she started to string together bits and pieces of a once-happy life.

After dinner, Daddy told Kate and me to clear the table and wash the dishes, but Mom wouldn't hear of it. "No, that's my job this weekend," she said. "I want the girls to be free of responsibility. I'm here to take the load off everyone." She wanted to relieve us of the burdens of the past, show us the competent, loving woman we had once known, and make this a seamless weekend—as if the fabric of our family had never been ripped apart.

Delighted with an unexpected reprieve from kitchen chores, I raced into the living room, sat on the floor in front of the TV, and watched *Dragnet*. Even then I was fascinated by the world of law and order, only I assumed that FBI agents and cops like Sergeant Friday were always right and told the truth. When there was a commercial break, I looked back and saw my parents sitting together on the couch, as they had in the old days. They didn't sit close, no part of one touched the other, but for a little while I let myself believe we were a family again.

On Saturday, Kate and I played jacks on the bathroom floor while Mom made pancakes and bacon, and Daddy read the sports page on the couch. After finishing her work in the kitchen, Mom made the beds and started sewing new nametags in our shirts and underwear. Daddy sat at his desk, made business calls for a while, and then took his pistol, a shiny, long-nosed German Luger, out of the safe and cleaned it.

Later that day, I sat on the kitchen counter and watched Mom iron some of our blouses. When that was done, she started preparing dinner, chopping carrots, onions, and potatoes and arranging them in the pressure cooker around a pot roast wrapped in string. She added a few cups of water and spices, then turned the lid until we heard it click into place.

Shortly after I left the kitchen to check on what Kate was up to, we smelled something burning. We raced to the kitchen and saw the iron, face down on my white blouse, and brown steam rising past the cabinets. Mom had gone to the bathroom and forgotten about the iron. "For goodness sake," she said when she returned, "I'm so sorry." She must have feared that her lapse in memory would be used as evidence that she was not ready to be freed from Camarillo.

As the afternoon wore on, the pungent aroma of the pot roast filled the apartment, and we heard a loud explosion in the kitchen. Powerful steam had blown the lid off the pot, and now our dinner was strewn across the ceiling, bits of greasy beef and potatoes dripping onto the floor. Mom covered her mouth with her hands. She had left the flame on medium instead of simmer.

Mom looked around at us with a despairing expression, retreated to the living room, and sat down in the rocking chair. I felt bad for her and sat cross-legged on the carpet in front of her. She seemed relieved to have the company and started asking me about what was happening in my life. Did I like it at Ramona Convent? Did I make friends there? What were my favorite TV shows? I chattered on as she rocked in the chair. I thought of cautioning her that one of the chair's wooden posts was loose, but with Mom in the chair, I didn't hear the usual squeaking that signaled a potential danger. All of a sudden, as she rocked backward, the chair tipped over, and she landed on her back, her legs straight up in the air, her girdle and garters exposed.

At first neither of us showed any reaction. Perhaps she feared that I saw the mishap as another example of her emotional instability, when actually the chair was—and had been for months—unstable. When I started laughing, she relaxed and joined in. "Well, I never," she said, laughing. "Imagine that." Our eyes filled with tears as the hilarity of the situation pushed us further into giddiness. Mom picked up the chair, straightened her hose, and winked at me. It was our secret.

Even then, at the age of ten, I was interested in the meaning of their sleeping arrangements. With only the one double bed in my father's room available to them, they would have to share it, and I wondered how he felt about that. Kate and I, lying in our twin beds, listened for sounds from the other room. We began whispering to each other.

"What do you think it means?" I asked, "that they're sleeping in the same bed?" Kate didn't seem much interested. "Shh," she said. "Not so loud. They'll hear us."

"Does it mean they're married again?"

"They're still married," Kate said. "They're just not together anymore."

I knew only the vaguest details about sex, just that it was something men and women did in private. And sleeping next to someone in the same bed, I thought, was as intimate as a man and woman could get. My hopes were buoyed again. Maybe they would get back together.

On Sunday, the realities of our lives began to return. In a few

hours Mom would return to Camarillo, and Kate and I would go
back to Ramona. Why, I wondered, did all the females in our family
have to live in institutions, and only Daddy got to live at home? But
it had been that way so long that it had begun to feel normal.

As I walked into their bedroom to see how Mom was holding
up, I saw her standing over Daddy's file cabinet. At first I couldn't
make out the object in her hand. Then I saw it was Daddy's pistol,
the German Luger. She was examining it carefully, turning it over
in her hands. When she noticed me, she pretended to finish dusting
it, then put it down carefully on the cabinet.

Should I run and tell my father, warn him that Mom was messing around with his gun? My first allegiance was to Daddy, and in
some strange, twisted way, I thought that tattling on Mom might
score me some points with him. But if I betrayed my mother, I might
never see her again. She must have thought she had failed a final test
that weekend, lost her last chance to regain her freedom and be re-
united with her children. So what was the point of going on? I knew
what the word *suicide* meant, but somehow, being such a dark and
frightening act, I didn't think it could ever apply to someone close to
me. Suicide only happened in books and to strangers.

In the end, I told no one about the incident.

We didn't see Mom again for two years, and it wasn't until I
was older that I learned why. When I thought about that weekend,
images of my mother holding the gun and Chirper stood out. A few
months after our reunion, when I came home from the convent,
Chirper's cage door was open and she was gone. Daddy said he had
been cleaning her cage outside, on the landing, when she flew away.
"Please tell me it's not true," I said. "Not again. Not Chirper!" How

could this have happened? I wondered if he had tired of cleaning her cage and had simply opened the cage door. He denied that, but it's the scenario that made the most sense. I missed Chirper terribly and worried she wouldn't survive in nature. I had heard somewhere that parakeets often didn't and either starved or were pecked to death by other birds.

As for images of my mother and the gun, it all made sense when Daddy finally told me the story of what had happened on their drive back to Camarillo that Sunday afternoon. Desperate not to return to the hospital, Mom tried to escape in the only way she knew how. They were heading back on the 101 Freeway, just past Cahuenga Pass, when my mother reached for her door handle. The next second, the door flew open and her body leaned halfway out of the car, about to fall into the path of the oncoming traffic. In a split second, my father reached over, grabbed Mom by the collar, and yanked her back in the car.

I almost wish he hadn't told me because the image of her dangling out of the car haunts me to this day.

15

Many kids grow up loving summer camp, but I wasn't one of them. I associated camp with unpleasant things like heat, mosquitoes, team sports, sunburn, and Mary Bertram, my father's new wife. I might have felt differently about camp had not my father, citing a busy work schedule, extended my stay at Ramona through a few summer sessions, which meant that during those years I lived at the convent all year round.

When I was eleven, my attitude about camp got even worse. A horse, mistaking my hair for hay, put his head over a fence and ate some of it. I saw how the horse could have mistaken my reddish-blond hair for straw, although that didn't speak well of its texture, which, admittedly, was on the dry side.

After that I didn't want to ride a horse ever again. But fear wasn't an acceptable excuse at Ramona, and Sister Rose Dominica made me get back in the saddle, which I suppose was the right thing to do. The horse walked for a few minutes and then, sensing my fear, took off, galloping away as I held on to the horn with both hands, screaming for help.

Volleyball presented another embarrassing dilemma. Earlier

that year, Daddy had taken me to the doctor when he noticed I had flat feet. Had we caught the problem earlier, the doctor said, he could have broken my arch bones and reset them, a grisly sounding surgery, but now all I could do was wear steel arch supports in my shoes. They were heavy metal supports that added at least a pound to each foot, and I walked as if I were struggling through a batch of wet concrete. I wasn't exactly prime athletic material, and when the volleyball captains picked their teams, I was always the last one sitting on the bench.

What I lacked in sports, I made up for in arts and crafts. In my first summer session at Ramona, the Sisters told us we could make anything we wanted—dolls, animals, bookmarks, cards, flowers— as long as we used the materials in the boxes they pulled out from storage. I rifled enthusiastically through the boxes and found wonderful scraps of felt, delicate lace, blue-and-white gingham, fun tassels, shiny sequins in silver and red, even some feathers, most likely taken from women's hats.

When I came across a strip of brown velvet, I got the idea to make a replica of Queenie and send it to Mom in the hospital. I'd use the brown velvet for her ears, a black button for her nose, a piece of white cotton for the tip of her tail, and plenty of batting to make her body round and plump.

"Who's that for?" a girl sitting across from me at the picnic table asked as Queenie began to take shape.

"My mother," I said proudly. "This used to be our dog."

"But you don't have a mother," the girl replied.

"I do, too!"

"You do not. Your mother's in the crazy house."

There it was, the truth, frozen in space. No one had ever spoken about her in that way, so directly, so callously, and I felt the breath rush from my body.

"What's going on here," Sister Rose Dominica asked when she saw me crying. I couldn't speak. To explain meant having to say the words out loud again. I picked up the unfinished remnants of Queenie and put them in the bottom drawer of my dresser, along with Mom's photo. It seemed that being her daughter had become a liability. I remember saying to myself that I would go back and finish sewing Queenie, but I never did.

So it goes without saying that camp was the last place I would have gone had I a choice in the matter. At the end of seventh grade, looking forward to spending the entire summer away from Ramona, I'd been home for only two weeks when Daddy sent me away again—to Camp Kiowa. It was Mary Bertram's idea. He had met her a year earlier at Tom Bergin's Tavern ("House of Irish Coffee"), his favorite bar and restaurant on Fairfax Avenue. Over the years it became his second home, and Tom Bergin, a kindly man with white hair, treated him like family. It was always dark inside the restaurant, even in the middle of the day. The bar was shaped like a horseshoe, and there were tables in the back for dining. For St. Patrick's Day, the bartenders grew beards and dyed them green, as they did the whipped cream for their famous Irish coffee. The walls were crammed with green paper shamrocks with the names of regular customers. The Fischer shamrock was hung near the end of the bar, high up over the cigarette machine, and when my father took us to Bergin's, I always checked to make sure our name hadn't faded.

My father said he'd been attracted to Mary right away, and when I met her at the beach one day, I could see why. She had dyed platinum, almost-white hair like Marilyn Monroe's, and when she stretched out on her blanket in the sand, her breasts spilled out of her one-piece bathing suit. Men looked her over when they passed by.

She was a professional hairdresser, divorced, with three children. She seemed nice enough, but like the other women before her, I figured she wouldn't last long. So there was no need to get to know her.

How wrong I was. That summer she came to live with us when her kids were in Phoenix visiting their father. It was a kind of trial between her and me, but it failed miserably after the first month. We fought like cats to mark our territory—my father. I didn't think it was fair that I had to share my home with a woman I hardly new and didn't much like. From her perspective as the adult, she thought I should kowtow to her.

"Now that's enough," my father said when he heard us arguing over who should fold the laundry. When the squabble didn't stop, he took her side and blamed me. He ordered me to lean over the side of his bed, pulled out his brown leather belt, and hit me, first to the right, then to the left, leaving a black-and-blue X on my bottom. I hated my father for that and wasn't sure I could, or would, ever love him again.

Mary called around until she found a solution—Camp Kiowa. It was the only one that would take such a late applicant, and the next thing I knew, I was headed for the San Bernardino Mountains and "beautiful Lake Elsinore," as the camp brochure described it. But when we got there, the lake was bone dry.

They married in 1964 and had their reception at Tom Bergin's, in the back dining room with the fireplace blazing. I put on the best face I could, but inside I was miserable. I was losing a father and gaining a stepmother who had it in for me. As I did for her. And on top of all that, we would now have to merge two distinct families under the guise of becoming one.

There were problems even before we moved in together. Daddy didn't want Mary's two older children—Caroline, age nineteen, and Peter, seventeen—to move in. He said Caroline was "loose" and ran around with a "bad crowd." As for Peter, he was big and hulking, with strong arms and a broad chest, and he wore white T-shirts like Marlon Brando in *On the Waterfront*. He oozed raw sexuality, and my father worried that he and Kate would end up having sex under his roof.

"These are my children you're talking about," Mary fumed. "Imagine if I spoke about your children that way. They're not perfect either, you know." But she finally relented.

That left her youngest daughter, also named Mary. She was twelve, two years younger than I was. In one fell swoop, I lost my favored position as the youngest child and had to share a bedroom with my new sister, a virtual stranger. What's more, I was no longer the only Mary in the family. There were now three of us, and to cut down on confusion, we took on our middle names: Mary Ellen, Mary Catherine, and Mary Alice.

In the beginning I shared Daddy's opinion that Mary Ellen's kids were lazy and ill mannered. When Peter came over for dinner (Daddy allowed him to do that occasionally), he talked with his mouth full and burped sometimes. "Hmm," Daddy said, raising his eyebrows. "Sounds like there's a pig in the house. Do you hear it, girls?" I loved that side of his sense of humor.

Instead of asking someone to pass the meat or peas, as Kate and I did, Peter and Mary Catherine reached over and took them. After dinner, when it was Mary Catherine's turn to do the dishes, she sometimes let them sit in the sink while she watched TV. That never bothered Mary Ellen—she sometimes did the dishes so her daughter wouldn't have to—but it infuriated my father.

"You see, this is what I mean," he said to her. "You're spoiling them. You're raising them to be slackers. Look at my kids. You don't see them slacking off."

I secretly enjoyed their fights. Kate and I were suddenly held up as paragons of what children should be, something we'd ordinarily never hear from my father. In time, though, I came to see that they were just being normal kids. We were the odd ones, raised like dutiful soldiers.

The arguments expanded to my souring relationship with Daddy's new wife. Not only had Mary Ellen become a rival for my father's attention, but she was not remotely like what I hoped for in a new mother. She could be loud and coarse, and she had no patience with me.

Even though I knocked before I entered their bedroom, she didn't like my coming in to say good night to my father. He didn't see the harm in it, but he went along with her wishes to keep peace. After she enrolled Mary Catherine at Ramona Convent, she would look out the living-room window to make sure I didn't always get to sit next to my father in his car.

Once, our bickering turned violent. I was in the den, lying on the couch reading, when she stormed in with round baking tins in each hand. For a minute I thought they were tambourines. "You call these clean?" she roared. "Look, just look at these pans. They're filthy!" It had been my turn that week to do the dishes, and I had missed a small smudge of grease on the bottom of one pan. Before I had a chance to fully inspect the other one, she took the tins and smashed them together on my hand.

"You have a black soul and you're going to hell!" she yelled. She had the look of a madwoman gone over the edge.

Her rage scared me, but I soon saw my advantage in the situation. Daddy would not take kindly to her prediction about the fate of my everlasting soul. And when I told him, he took my side for the first time. "Don't you ever touch my child again," he said to Mary Ellen.

Home became a war zone, and I took to hiding in the coat closet. Even Christmas provided no peace. When it was time to decorate the tree, Mary Ellen instructed Mary Catherine to hang their family ornaments, but my father countermanded her and told me to put up ours. Back and forth we went, from the tree to the boxes of ornaments, first taking them out and then putting them back. They eventually compromised and used some of both, but deciding on which ornament to use on top—the angel or the star—was our undoing. After I put the Fischer star on the tip and climbed down the ladder, Mary Ellen told her daughter to go back up, take the star down, and put up their angel. Halfway up the ladder, she fell into the tree and tipped it over.

Despite all the commotion around me, I felt lonely and got the urge to have another pet. It had been four years since Chirper and nothing since then. Dogs were out of the question, I knew that. Too much responsibility, my father said. I dare not get another bird or goldfish for fear of what might happen to them. And, I didn't want a pet that I would get too attached to, so I got a turtle and named him Peppy.

Peppy's bowl was plastic, with a small ramp and palm tree on top. I put the bowl over the credenza by the breakfast room window so the sun could stream in on him. The clerk at the pet store had told me that sunshine would keep his shell hard. I loved it when Peppy used the ramp and sat in the mixed-color gravel, as if sunning himself on a rock in Hawaii. When I came home from Ramona for a visit, I would take him outside in the sun and let him crawl around on the grass, free to waddle wherever he pleased.

The clerk had also told me that small turtles like Peppy rarely lived very long, but I didn't pay any attention to that. A few months later he died, and when I came home and saw his empty bowl, I realized how attached I had become to him.

Soon after that, Mary Ellen and my father divorced. The marriage had lasted two years—about a year longer than it should have—and all of us were relieved. My father said it hadn't worked because of all the children. "The only thing they had in common was that they all had one head," he used to tell people.

It always seemed strange to me that after living closely under one roof, after sharing countless meals, our birthdays, the holidays, after living like a family, even a troubled one, I never saw any of them again.

16

One good thing about Ramona Convent for me was that it went up to only the eighth grade. So when I graduated, I was finally free to leave—for good—and live at home with my father. Just saying the words—*live at home*—felt as if I were going some place exciting, an unexplored destination, almost exotic because of how foreign the experience was for me.

As we started our high-school years, Kate and I settled into a new life with a single father who had returned to his bachelor ways and had two philosophies about child rearing: Do what I say, not what I do, and his revision of the old Victorian adage, which was, Children should not be seen or heard. We thought he was kidding then, but at his core I believe he wished it could have been that way.

I know he loved us, but he had no clue about how to raise children. He provided the basics—food, shelter, clothing, and presents at Christmas and on our birthdays. But beyond that he was lost. Raised in an era when men were expected to hide their emotions, he didn't know what "emotional needs" meant. Praise, guidance, nurturing, support, and involvement were not part of his parental repertoire. The key to turning out fine, upstanding children, he used to say, was making them "toe the line." He expected us to be perfect, and when we weren't, he let us know with criticism.

He had two pieces of advice for us: "A woman can never have too many black cocktail dresses" and "Don't just get married and have a family. Look what happened to your mother. Find a good career and make something of your life."

By the time he enrolled us in Immaculate Heart High School, Daddy was on a roll. His real estate business had finally taken off, and he could now live the "high life" he felt entitled to. No more used cars and cheap apartments. He paid cash for a brand-new metallic green Cadillac convertible, the model with the long pointed fins, and joined the Del Mar Beach Club, and we moved to a beautiful and spacious Spanish-style duplex in Hancock Park. He hired an interior decorator and bought new furniture.

Daddy took the master bedroom that had an adjoining bathroom. Instead of choosing the next-largest bedroom, which would have been Kate's prerogative, being the oldest, she chose the small, plain maid's room in back of the kitchen, off the laundry room. She wanted to be as far away from Daddy and me as possible—"removed from the field of battle," she said.

Now that we were both at home—"underfoot" as Daddy put it—he installed bolt locks on the inside of his bedroom and bathroom doors, his "private quarters." We thought it was odd at first; none of the parents we knew locked their children out. But when we thought about it more, we saw it worked both ways. We could keep him from barging in on us, and we put locks on the inside of our bedroom doors.

We didn't so much live together as we had sparring matches in our communal boxing ring. We'd come together for meals or when we had company, but then, after a few rounds of back-and-forth barbs and teasing, or Daddy's threats to take away our privileges for one infraction or another, we would retreat to our respective corners and lock ourselves in our bedrooms. I felt safe in my room, knowing that no one could enter without my permission, and that made me feel grown up. When Daddy knocked and demanded that I unlock the door, I would call out, "What do you want? I'm busy!" I savored the brief moments when I had control over my own life.

At dinnertime we came out for another round. A certain amount of cunning and dexterity was essential if you wanted to get enough to eat at our house. We said grace, put our napkins in our laps, picked up our forks, and made small talk, and by then my father and I had already planned our first moves. Casually, as if it were hardly worth mentioning, I'd say to him, "Look, you just spilled some peas." If I was lucky, I'd catch him off guard and he would look down at his lap. Then I would quickly reach over with my fork and spear his ham or sausage from his dish. He was a skillful faker and would soon retaliate when I least expected it. With an equally casual remark, he would nab my food when I looked up or out the window.

We loved the game, but Kate considered it beneath her. She would either refuse to join in or just ignore us. "You're such heathens," she would say, and then one of us would spear food from her plate. The game solidified our roles—my father the supreme instigator, me his devilish collaborator, Kate the tortured outsider.

Daddy and I could just as easily be adversaries as collaborators. When I challenged his unfair rules, his stubbornness and remoteness, we met on the field of battle, face-to-face, my David to his Goliath, arguing with him, questioning his logic, and in those rounds, I think he gained respect for me.

Sometimes my boldness worked and I got him to relent. Other times, as with the phone, I made things worse.

We were not allowed to talk on the phone for longer than five minutes. He would clock us, using the egg timer. Sometimes I would successfully distract him, usually by handing him the day's mail and then turning the timer upside down. Eventually, when Kate and I began working summer jobs, Daddy agreed to let us get our own phone on the condition that it have a jack. That way, he could unplug it and still retain some measure of control over our phone privileges. When he wanted our attention, or felt we had not spent sufficient time cleaning our rooms, he would remove our phone and lock it in his closet. That drove us mad.

"It's not fair that you do that," I told him one day. "We're paying the bill, not you. How would you feel if we did that to your phone?" He knew I was right but remained intractable.

We were not allowed to date or wear makeup. That wasn't a problem for me. I was only marginally interested in boys then, but it became a problem for Kate. When she wanted to see a boy, I helped her sneak out and meet him at her friend Lynn's house. In case Daddy might check her room, I would make her bed to look like she was in it, with pillows rumpled under the blankets and a wig on her pillow.

Immaculate Heart was another all-girls Catholic school, but the Sisters were far more progressive than the nuns at Ramona. They encouraged individual expression through the school's art, drama, and public-speaking classes, and on Fridays they let us abandon our navy-blue–and-white uniforms and wear "free dress." If they had taught school in the 1800s, they probably would have been burned at the stake for their liberal ideas.

When I was there, the bright, bold lithography of the renowned artist Sister Corita Kent hung all around the campus, with hip messages like WE CAN CREATE LIFE WITHOUT WAR. LOVE IS HERE TO STAY AND THAT'S ENOUGH. In the seventies, during the reformist period of Vatican II, the nuns defied the church hierarchy by refusing to wear habits anymore. Cardinal McIntyre banished them from the archdiocese, and that only endeared them to us more.

The student body was a mix of girls from middle-class and wealthy families who lived in huge Hancock Park mansions, some with so many bathrooms the girls sometimes didn't know the exact number. Today the school can boast about the would-be celebrities who attended it over the years: Natalie, the daughter of Nat King Cole; Mary Tyler Moore; Hollywood madam Heidi Fleiss; and the model Tyra Banks.

Most of the girls had more money and clothes than me, but those distinctions paled in comparison to the biggest difference: I was surrounded by girls from traditional families. Both parents lived at home, their mothers were homemakers, their fathers the sole breadwinners, and on Sundays they went to Mass together.

By then my father no longer went to church—he had failed to keep his end of our bargain—but he expected Kate and me to go. He'd drop us off at Cathedral Chapel two miles from our house, then go to places we never knew, and return in an hour to pick us up. Before he got the Cadillac, he used to wait for us in the parking lot in his old white Ford station wagon, a beat-up relic parked amid shiny, elegant cars of people like the Cavanaughs and the Calhouns. When we came out of church, Daddy sometimes had the hood hiked up and would be poking the engine with a long wood pole, trying to get it started, which embarrassed Kate and me no end.

In our neighborhood the parents formed a car pool and took

turns driving their kids to school. Mothers of my friends usually picked us up, and we could count on the twenty-minute drive being safe and uneventful. When it was my father's turn, I prayed to be sick or invisible so I'd be spared the embarrassment of his antics. He liked driving with the top down on his Cadillac and made a point of turning the radio to KFWB, the cool station. He often got the girls' names mixed up. "Good morning, Sally," he'd say as Elaine or Ann climbed into the backseat. "Daddy!" I'd say, mortified.

When he picked up everyone and the car was full of girls, the car radio would be blaring with music by the Beatles or the Rolling Stones, and he would sing along, messing up most of the lyrics. When the light turned green at an intersection, he would sometimes floor the gas pedal and off we'd go with tires screeching on the asphalt. The girls would squeal and beg for more.

Those were among his happiest moments. A car full of girls having a great time, our long hair blowing in the open air. He loved to have people watching him from their cars or the sidewalk, perhaps envying him for his fast, elegant car, his boldness and position as one man among so many females.

None of my friends ever came to my house, and I couldn't figure out why at first. I frequently went to Ann Cavanaugh's house for dinner, and every so often I spent the night. When I went, I became quiet and reserved, as if I had entered a sacred museum where I could observe the workings of a regular family. I felt like an outsider, the way I imagined Oliver Twist must have felt when, standing on a street corner in the cold wet of a London winter, he looked into a window in the distance and saw a big family sitting down to a sumptuous feast.

I was enthralled with the Cavanaugh's cohesiveness, how they sat at the table, or in the den, together, just talking. They talked about such things as their last camping trip in the desert and their plans to go to Yellowstone Park next year. Mr. Cavanaugh knew a lot about the interests of his daughter Ann. He knew she loved Robaire, their oversexed toy poodle who humped my leg every time I came over, and he allowed the dog to sleep on Ann's bed and sit with her on the couch. Mr. Cavanaugh knew, too, that his daughter was shy and preferred to be with one friend rather than a group, so he didn't force her to join school clubs. He also knew what kind of car she wanted when she could legally own and drive one, so he gave her a T-Bird on her eighteenth birthday.

I loved it when Mrs. Cavanaugh, for no apparent reason, pinched Ann's cheek and called her "my Mariuch." She understood what her daughter needed in the way of clothes, even before the girl knew herself.

When I would invite Ann or Maggie Calhoun to my house, they would always say they were too busy to come over. They never mentioned it had anything to do with my mother not being there. In fact, they never mentioned my mother, nor did I. Friends would later tell me that they thought my mother was dead because I never talked about her. To further disconnect from her, and the inherited destiny I feared, I ironed my hair to get the wave out and drenched it with hydrogen peroxide, turning it into orange straw. To hide the hideous results, I had to wear scarves for weeks.

Finally I learned that my friends' parents didn't trust our family arrangement: a single, socially active man, alone at the house with no wife on the scene. Only my friend Sue Liberti would occasionally come to dinner. Her mother was a widow on disability and didn't keep close tabs on Sue, which was probably a mistake. Daddy always liked having Sue around. I thought it was because she was friendly and outgoing, but it was more than that. He liked to flirt with her, and she knew how to flirt back. Sue was way out of my league. Even at sixteen she was physically mature beyond her years and fully confident about her emerging womanhood.

But one day, as we got older, Daddy became more aware of Sue's voluptuous body in a tight skirt and said to me, "She's not the kind of girl I want you to associate with. She's much too wild for you."

17

For my sixteenth birthday, Daddy took Kate and me to the Moulin Rouge nightclub on Sunset Strip in Hollywood. "A special birthday requires a special celebration," he said. From his perspective as a single man who loved the nightlife, he could think of no better coming-of-age than to take his daughters to one of his swanky haunts. He had no interest in a traditional, sweet-sixteen celebration, which was a big relief to me. The thought of my father officiating at the kind of party Ann had had the month before—a party in the elegant tearoom of Saks Fifth Avenue, complete with scones and cucumber-and-salmon sandwiches with the crust cut off—was as odd to me as it was to him. I could just see Daddy sitting at the head of a long table full of giggling girls, smoking cigarettes as he nursed his drinks and flirted with the more mature girls.

For my party, I wore a midnight-blue taffeta dress with a full skirt that came just below my knees (which fit Immaculate Heart High School's dress code), a high neck with a scalloped collar, and a small bow in the center that made me look hopelessly prim and girlish. The worst part about the dress was the bodice: It fit snugly around my chest and revealed to all the world how flat chested I was.

Even though I owned a bra, my first, and wore it that night, the extra fabric adding a hint of rumpled roundness to my bust, I didn't actually need one. But that was beside the point. As more and more of my classmates "filled out" that sophomore year and their mothers took them to buy bras, I felt conspicuous not wearing one, and feared they would ridicule me if they found out. I asked Kate to go with me to buy one, but she said she was too busy. "Besides, you don't even need one," she said.

I got the bra just before Christmas, when Ann's mother, Mrs. Cavanaugh, took me shopping. She was the perfect emissary for the mission, authoritative yet aware of a young girl's feelings. "It's all right, dear," she said, patting me as we approached the lingerie department. I stood back with hunched-up shoulders and bowed my head as she chatted with the saleslady and told her what I needed. The lady looped a yellow measuring tape around my chest and looked at me from the front and side, as if evaluating a cow she was considering buying, and announced her findings. I needed a 32AA bra, the smallest size they carried.

When I showed Kate the bra, I made her swear not to tell Daddy, but he found out on his own on Christmas Eve. We usually went out to dinner on the holidays, and that year we met some of his buddies and their wives at the Ambassador Hotel, one of the city's oldest and most elegant hotels, which became the landmark where Robert F. Kennedy was shot.

We were standing in the foyer, waiting to be seated in the large dining room, when someone in our group complimented me on my gold brocade dress, which they said made me look "so pretty and grown up." I knew the dress was unflattering, stiff and gaudy like a hotel bedspread, but I welcomed the compliment. Something about it triggered my father's dark side and he struck, like a snake that suddenly appears when a rock is overturned. He pulled out the front of my dress, glanced down my chest, and, upon seeing my bra, joked, "Well, what do we have here? You don't need a bra, Mary."

Everyone in the group was stunned, and I, standing there in a circle of adults, shrinking in humiliation, began to cry. I wanted to run away so I would never see my father or these people ever again. I settled for the ladies' room. How could I ever look them in the face again?

During dinner I sulked and spoke only when it was necessary to order my meal. At home later that night, Daddy apologized, but I couldn't bring myself to forgive him. As always, he offered no explanation for his insensitive remarks. I spent most of Christmas Day in my room, sulking and staring at the ceiling, sunk deep in thought. There must be something wrong with me to invite such insults—the conclusion I always reached when Daddy lobbed criticisms at me. I could not deflect his cruelty, could not hold my own in his complicated psychological game that had no winners.

K ate's encounters with Daddy about her emerging womanhood differed from mine, but they were no less humiliating. On the night of my birthday, she wore a sleeveless black sheath dress that showed off her shapely figure, making it clear she had taken seriously my father's favorite dictum about women and black cocktail dresses. She wore black high heels and small pearl earrings, and she rolled her hair up in a French twist secured with sticky hair spray.

She looked more like a woman than a girl in her last year in high school. We didn't realize it at the time, but both of us dressed in ways we thought would please Daddy and secure our place in his life. Our different styles reflected his view of us. Kate was the mature one, the adult who would look after me when he wasn't home. She wore feminine things and acted like a grown-up lady, believing—though she would never admit it—that her appearance appealed to her father's appreciation of attractive women.

At times he complimented the way she dressed, and at other times he criticized her. I think it somehow threatened him, knowing that she would soon replace him with another man and have no need for him anymore, because of some of the things he told her. "You can't go out looking like that," he said once, when Kate wore a short dress that came above her knees. "You look cheap."

Another time, as she was getting ready for some important event, and told him she wanted "to look her best," he replied, "Well, yes, of course, but you're not a pretty girl." And the strange thing is that she *was* a pretty girl, but she bowed her head, dejected and sad, and said, "I know, but I still want to look my best."

For my part, I dared not grow up, so I wore young girl's outfits. I was Daddy's little girl, the one who adored and waited on him, and if he saw I was becoming a woman, he'd have no need for me. That's how I saw things.

On the way to the Moulin Rouge that night, we drove down Sunset Strip in my father's Cadillac, past strip clubs with neon lights flashing women's gyrating bodies, past the billboard of the giant Marlboro Man, the famous Scandia restaurant where the TV series *77 Sunset Strip* was filmed. It was all so magical and exciting, being out on a Friday night in the most famous part of the city.

A few blocks east of the Brown Derby restaurant, we pulled into the club's driveway. My father didn't need an introduction. Everyone knew him. "Good evening, Mr. Fischer," the parking valet said as he opened my father's door first, then came around and opened ours.

Inside, the maître d' in a black tuxedo came to attention. "Ah, Mr. Fischer," he said, bowing as if greeting a king. "Good evening. So good to see you again. So which one of these pretty girls is having a birthday?"

"I am," I said, raising my hand as I did to confirm my attendance in class.

"Well, then," he said, "we'll make sure it's a memorable birthday." Daddy's prestige and valued patronage had allowed us in the club on the condition that his daughters would consume no alcohol and remain in their seats the whole time we were there. I suspect he also paid the owner a handsome fee.

Scanning the club, I saw small round tables full of well-dressed men and women, couples mostly, drinking and smoking cigarettes, their smoke swirling in the air. Kate and I walked on either side of Daddy with our arms looped as we followed the maître d' down the aisle toward the stage. I felt proud, like the Red Sea had parted to make way for us.

As we took our seats, I noticed people looking at us. Some smiled, appreciating no doubt the novelty of a father out on the town with his two daughters. I was obviously his daughter, but some of the people there may have thought that Kate, the older girl with the French twist in her dark hair, could be his date.

Daddy ordered a martini, straight up, with three green olives. The extra one was for me. "And, my man," he said to the waiter with a slight English accent, "my daughters here will have a Shirley Temple." Kate scowled. She didn't want such a childish drink, and changed her order to ginger ale.

A few minutes later, the club went dark. Over the stage, from somewhere in the ceiling, a light went on, casting a large oval shape on the barren floor. Everyone looked up. Something big but as yet undefined was up there. Then, slowly, an oversized champagne glass, the size of a small tree, descended from the ceiling. As it dropped lower, I could hardly believe what I saw. A slender, naked woman sat in the center of the glass, her shapely legs crossed provocatively so you could almost see up between her legs. I felt my cheeks flushing, but the darkness hid my embarrassment.

Upon closer look, I saw that the woman wasn't completely naked. She had on a see-through, flesh-colored leotard, and her nipples and pubic area were covered, though just barely, with small gold sparkles.

I looked over at Daddy to see if he was annoyed or embarrassed for us, but he smiled straight ahead, as if her act were the most normal thing in this world. When the champagne glass finally settled on the stage, the woman stepped out gracefully, opened her arms and bowed to the audience, then continued to strut around the stage, her bottom completely bare. When she came around to our table, she smiled at us, and I noticed how beautiful she was—the epitome of what a woman should be, at least in my father's eyes.

I didn't know the first thing about what it meant to be a woman. At sixteen, I felt neuter, in a coma from the neck down. I knew virtually nothing about what dresses to wear or how best to style my hair. My periods had started a few months before, so technically I was a woman, but in no other way did I feel like one.

It happened one afternoon after I'd come home from school and was sitting in the living room listening to Beatles records. I became aware of something warm oozing between my legs. *Oh no,* I thought, *it can't be.* But it was. Who should I tell? What should I do?

I certainly couldn't tell my father, and I was afraid Kate would just laugh. Finally I called my friend Sue Liberti, and she asked her mother to go out and buy me a box of Kotex. "I don't understand how it works," I told Mrs. Liberti over the phone. "Well, take a pad out of the box," she said, "and I'll walk you through it. There's nothing to it."

What did it mean to be a woman? I had no role model to guide me, except for Daddy's girlfriends, who never stuck around very long. What was there to recommend it? In my mind there was more bad than good. Women got cramps, their breasts swelled and got sore, they married young, gave up their dreams, and stretched their bellies out having children. They stayed at home doing housework, wiping off dirty bottoms, and cooking, while their husbands were out in the world, meeting interesting people, having lunch in nice restaurants. As women got older, they were lucky if their husbands didn't leave them for younger women. And if they did, well, then, a breakdown might follow. Then they got old, their skin sagged, they lost their looks, and that was the end of it.

As the evening ended and we drove home, I sorted through my feelings: excited, proud, a bit ashamed, yet I settled on feeling grateful for having been invited into my father's private world, the place where he was happiest and most at ease. I loved seeing that he had had such a good time—with his daughters by his side.

1 8

My father picked up women as easily as most men pick up the morning newspaper. He met them in bars and restaurants, at football games, in the supermarket. Once, I heard he had even met a woman on the Hollywood Freeway. He was in his Cadillac with the top down. She was in a blue Oldsmobile. They smiled and nodded at each other for a few miles, then Daddy motioned for her to pull off to the side so they could chat and exchange phone numbers. Very likely that led to another of his affairs.

Daddy had a magical effect on women—of all ages, it seemed. When he was seventeen, in his junior year at Hamilton Catholic High School, an attractive woman in her thirties, smitten with my father, used to pick him up after school. It was the talk of Hamilton. People wanted to know the nature of their relationship and whether they had sex, but all he said was "There's nothing going on."

In many ways he was a catch. He was confident in most any situation, witty, playful, charming, and handsome. He took his dates to nice places, always paid the bill, and more than one told me he was a good lover.

All through my high-school years, a parade of attractive women came and went from our apartment. Some were respectable, up-standing women like Abby, my favorite, who dressed with class and never used bad language. Others were like Helen, easy and on the cheap side, with obviously bleached hair, too much black eye-liner, and low-cut blouses and sweaters that showed off their ample cleavage.

Most of them were in their thirties, but once he invited a twenty-five-year-old woman over, only seven more than Kate. When she learned of it, she called the affair a disgrace, but I thought it was cool. Here was my father, in his fifties, still able to attract beautiful young women.

They all had one thing in common—they never lasted very long. I might see them once or twice, maybe three times, and then never again. Naively I assumed Daddy was looking for love, some-one special to settle down with again, and he just hadn't found the right woman yet.

At first Daddy never brought his dates home. He had two lives—one with us and the other out on the town. His dates knew that two teenage daughters lived with him, but seeing us in the flesh, making his encumbered home life all too real, might "gum up the works"—his term for anything that interfered with his sex life.

He went out three or four nights a week, usually to Tom Bergin's. As he got ready to go, I would sit on the edge of his bed and offer advice on what he should wear. It gave me an opportunity to be close to him. But these were bittersweet moments—although they were among our most intimate, I was helping him leave me home alone yet again.

Our playful ritual always began the same way. After he had splashed aftershave lotion on his face and neck, he put on a crisp, starched shirt, white or light blue, then picked out a suit from his closet. "What tie should I wear with this?" he would ask. I loved being consulted and took my assignment seriously. He had at least twenty-five ties hanging in his closet, and the fine silk ones had cost plenty. I let them fall slowly through my fingers, paying close attention to what colors and design would go best with the suit he had selected. I usually picked two so he could make the final decision. If I picked one he didn't like, I feared he would lose faith in my judgment and never ask for my advice again.

"Now, what about cuff links?" he asked. He probably already knew which pair he wanted to wear, but I went to his dresser and opened his mahogany jewelry box, lined in black velvet, and carefully scanned his collection. I knew he loved his gold nugget cuff links best, so I usually selected them.

When he was almost ready to go, our banter began. "Where are you going, Daddy?" I asked as he put on his jacket.

"Going out to the library to do some research," he said with a smirk.

"Then I'll come with you," I said, baiting him.

"No," he said. "This is research I have to do alone."

I watched from the living-room window as he drove away in his Cadillac, and several hours later I heard him stumble up the stairs, either alone or with a new woman he'd just met. If I never saw his dates a second or third time, that was fine with me. I didn't want to share what little I had of him—what little he could give—with anyone else.

After about a year, Daddy began inviting his dates over for drinks before they went out to dinner. Kate wasn't interested in meeting them. She might say hello as she passed through the living room, but then she'd retreat to her bedroom and lock herself in. I was deeply curious and made a point of sticking around for as long as Daddy would allow it. The women were rivals for my father's love and attention, and I wanted to see whom I was dealing with.

He had constructed a makeshift bar out of an old headboard that he set up, with bar stools, in a corner of the dining room. He added two shelves that he stocked with liquor and cocktail glasses of various sizes, two silver jiggers, and a blender for margaritas and daiquiris.

Drawing on my earlier experience from our barbecues in the Valley, I would step in as the bartender. I figured I'd be in the center of things and could learn more about his dates.

For margaritas, I cracked ice cubes in the palm of my hand with the back of a tablespoon, just as Daddy had taught me. For whiskey sours, I cut an orange into slim sections and set them on the rim of the glass. When it came to martinis, one of my father's favorite drinks, I almost never lived up to his high standards. I would chill the glasses first, then carefully measure one jigger of vodka, one jigger of vermouth, and a few ice shavings into the silver mixer, and then shake it. My father said I must have "bruised" the martinis because they tasted "off."

Still, as his dates sat on the bar stool, I could tell they were impressed with my skills. What a novelty for a young girl to be such a good bartender. Then they would look at my father with respect and appreciation. Here was a single father raising two such charming, well-behaved daughters on his own.

Abby was my favorite among Daddy's dates. She was warm and kind, the only one who gave me extra attention. Tall and thin, with chestnut-colored, shoulder-length hair, she looked a little like Lauren Bacall. The others were nice, but they only asked me silly questions about how old I was and what grade I was in. When Abby asked how things were going in my life, she seemed genuinely interested. She wanted to know about my friends, if I was interested in any boys. "You can tell me," she said. "I won't tell your father."

I liked her so much that I sewed a muumuu for her. It was the easiest thing I could make without screwing things up, and I thought it would please her. It took longer than I expected—two weeks—mainly because I messed up the stitching around the dropped neckline and had to start over. Abby hugged me when I gave it to her and wore it the next time she came over.

Then, all of a sudden, she vanished, and I never saw her again. Gone, just like a snap of the fingers. "But why?" I kept asking Daddy. "She was so nice. She's the best. I wouldn't even mind if you married her."

"Some things you just wouldn't understand," he said.

In time, he took the next step and began bringing some of his dates back home to spend the night. That's when my investigative skills were first honed. I was usually asleep when they returned at one or two in the morning, but their voices woke me up and I listened to their whispers as they climbed up the stairs. Sometimes one or both of them were drunk, and they banged into walls and broke out laughing.

When I heard Daddy push the bolt lock into the latch on his bedroom door, I climbed out of bed and crouched down next to the heater vent, which connected to the vent in his bathroom, giving me a direct line for eavesdropping. My motives were mixed. As an innately curious person, I wanted details, the facts, so I could further assess whether my father was serious about any particular woman. And I also wanted to know what went on between men and women. What little I knew about courtship and sex came from my friends, although they were just as ignorant about it. But we were all damned curious.

Once I heard Helen, one of Daddy's girlfriends, splashing around in his bathtub, and from the sounds I thought he must be sitting on the edge of the tub and washing her back. In the morning I heard the lock on his door slide open, which meant the coast was clear and I could go in. The bed was made, so there was no direct evidence of their having slept together. Daddy sat in his green leather chair sipping coffee while Helen lounged on the bed polishing her nails.

After we were introduced to each other, I asked Helen, "Did you just get here this morning?" I was trying to find out whether they'd had sex.

"Your father invited me," she said. "I'm here because he asked me. And you'd better get used to it. I'm going to marry him."

"Oh yeah," I said. Like I was a tough guy. "We'll see about that!"

My father shot me what he intended as a disapproving look, but it was more like stunned amusement. Then I knew she didn't have a prayer with him, and I never saw Helen again.

The story behind how my father met his fourth wife begins in my junior year in high school when I enrolled in an elective typing class. My job skills were limited, and the way things were going at home, I figured I might need to get a job. The real estate market had slowed to its lowest level in a decade, and several of Daddy's big deals had fallen through and he was in debt. He was in between wives, and creditors called the house looking for him. "Is this the Fischer residence?" they'd ask.

"No, sorry, you have the wrong number," I'd say and hang up. When I came home from school, I often found Daddy slumped in his green leather chair, starring at a blank TV screen. He drank more during those days, and his face flared up with blotchy impetigo, a sure sign he was in distress.

One day Kate and I came home and found him selling off the expensive furniture and paintings he'd bought a few years before, when he was flush. We were desperate to hang on to our favorite pieces, so later that night, after he'd gone out to Tom Bergin's restaurant, we carried out the carved-wood Chinese chest and my bedroom mirror down the backstairs and hid them under a blanket in the back of the garage.

In my typing class the typewriters were huge, heavy monstrosities that would break your foot if they fell on you. At the end of the semester, Sister Eulalia gave us a five-minute typing test. Whoever typed the fastest with the fewest mistakes would win a summer typing job at the phone company. We all typed furiously for five minutes straight, the bells of our return carriages pinging wildly. "All right, now stop!" Sister said.

With ninety words per minute and only two mistakes, I won, and the class dubbed me Fire Fingers. It turned out to be a dubious victory. That summer I worked in the order room of the phone company in Hollywood. Day after day I typed for eight hours straight—all kinds of customer orders on a behemoth Teletype machine. I used part of my salary to help Daddy handle our bills at home. I paid the milkman, the electric bill, and the tuition for my last semester in high school.

"I want you to know I appreciate this, sweetheart," he said, hugging me. "I'll pay you back." And he did.

Joanne Morris, a gracious, attractive woman always impeccably groomed, was my training supervisor at the phone company. She had her hair done at a beauty parlor once a week and dressed in beautiful suits and dresses, most of which she made herself. She had been married once to an FBI agent who ended up "boring" her, so they divorced.

My father hadn't been out on a date in a while. He couldn't afford them. Things were that bad. I thought he desperately needed a good woman, stable and solvent, who could pull him out of the quicksand. So I set him up with Joanne on a blind date, drove him in my used but dashing red MG convertible, which I had bought myself. When we got to her apartment, I introduced them, then left them alone and went home.

They seemed to hit it off. One night when they were sitting in the living room, I listened from behind my bedroom door. They were talking about getting married—my father had proposed a few months before—but there was one impediment. Me. Joanne had no children of her own and didn't want any now. Kate had already moved out, so Daddy's decision about marrying her, I thought, would tell me where I stood. He would have to choose between us.

Then my outlook shifted, and I viewed the situation in a more practical way. If I tried to stand in the way of their marriage, I would truly be the impediment to my father's salvation. So I moved out and rented a room for sixty dollars a month in the home of Elaine's parents three miles away.

I cried myself to sleep the first few nights. It felt strange being in another family's home in an unfamiliar bed, having to be formal, putting on my best manners all the time. *But at least now my father can be happy,* I thought.

They married a few months later, shortly after my eighteenth birthday. This time I had given Daddy away in order to save him. I was their witness and maid of honor at the wedding. As I stood at my father's side on the steps of the altar, I felt glad that he would be loved, and sad that I would be losing him again. Kate sat in the first pew holding a Kleenex in her hands, trying to hide her tears.

part two Bail

Free at last. Mom and me at her wedding in 1981.

19

Whenever I see a movie with a scene of an inmate walking out of prison after serving a long sentence, I think of my mother and the day she was finally released from Camarillo in late 1964. I didn't know she was getting out and thus couldn't be there to meet her, but I like to think a beautiful day, warm and bright, greeted her as she walked out of that place for the last time. After nine long years locked away from the world, it must have seemed unreal to her, knowing she was free at last. Now she could make her own decisions about where she went, how she dressed, what she ate—all that she had once taken for granted.

Her elation must have blended with fear that day. She was fifty-three, the age when many people were thinking of winding down, and now she was starting over with virtually nothing. Her life would not be remotely as it had once been. There was no house, no stylish clothes anymore. No fine china or pressed linen napkins. No barbecues and parties. No place to live, no job, no family to speak of. Her parents were dead, her husband long gone, and her daughters all but gone in terms of how little we had communicated with her over the last few years.

When she tried to get a job, what could she put in a résumé? That she'd been an exceptional mother and homemaker? That she used to type her husband's letters, make piecrust from scratch, and could pull together a respectable dinner in thirty minutes? And how would she account for the past nine years? A former mental patient wasn't exactly what prospective employers were looking for.

She was starting over with a few creased photographs of her parents and Kate and me when we were little, and two small suitcases that contained all of her possessions. The heavy verbal baggage would come later—the scorn, the shame, the harsh judgments of those people who would pull away and suddenly be too busy when they found out where she had been for nearly a decade.

When Mom got out of the hospital, the world had changed in ways she couldn't recognize. A new culture of permissiveness and nonconformity had emerged, and the conventional values of the fifties were now passé. She began her new life in the sixties, in the middle of a revolution of spirit, of consciousness, of race, and of music. A time like no other, when traditional institutions were falling apart and the old social order, everything it stood for, was dying.

How would a relic from a different era find her way, how would she fit in? Even the language and fashion had changed dramatically. What was a *hippie*? she wondered. What was this about "dropping out" or "waging war against the military-industrial complex." When a person said, "I am Somebody, I am a Man," what did he mean?

Mom told us later that she might not have been released for at least several more years had not a Camarillo psychologist, Dr. Goodman, taken an interest in her case. The irony of his name didn't escape her. It took a "good man" to finally recognize that she didn't belong there anymore. The first doctor to pay any real attention to her, he watched her interact with other patients and the staff, around the pool, at picnics, in the cafeteria. Everyone she came in contact with liked her. She had a gentle, healing effect on the other patients and often made them laugh. He saw something special in Mom and worked to get her released.

My father told a different story. Mom, he said, started "to snap out of it" only after he filed for divorce. He had held off because of a law in California that made it illegal to divorce a spouse committed to a mental institution—a protection against one-sided legal proceedings. But once the law changed in 1964, he immediately filed for divorce. That gave Mom a strong dose of reality, he theorized, finally cracking her illusion that she might be able to hang on to him if she stayed in the hospital.

Without Dr. Goodman's intervention, Mom could have languished in Camarillo for three more years, until 1967, when the landmark Lanterman-Petris-Short law was passed. It was the first in a series of reformist laws that brought the mental health field out of the shadows and into the modern day. Patients were given more rights and control over their treatment, and the laws did away with the tradition of warehousing patients for long periods of time. Now the focus was on treatment that would get patients back into society as soon as possible.

Dr. Goodman also helped Mom prepare to leave Camarillo. She needed someone to sign her out and take responsibility for her until she got on her feet. The doctor called my father and asked if he would do it. He considered it, for about a minute, and then declined. It had been a long haul, and now it was time to cut the cord and move on with his own life. But he did offer to give Mom some money and contact her cousin Marshall McCoy in Kansas.

To many people, including me, the town of Oxnard doesn't sound like an appealing place to live, certainly not a place Mom ever would have picked had her life not taken a bad turn. To begin with, there's the name Oxnard. "It's like getting down castor oil," a longtime resident told me. "You just have to say it." When you do, the name conjures up images of stockyards; old, broken-down oxen pulling hay trucks; dirt fields; open-bed trucks. It sounded like a town for the hay-and-pitchfork crowd, not the sophisticated kind of places where Mom had once lived.

Pulled between fear and love, Mom wanted to live in Los Angeles so she would be close to Kate and me, but after a discussion with her cousin Marshall, she chose Oxnard, a small town next to Camarillo where she could get her bearings. It was founded by five entrepreneurial families, including the Henry Oxnards from the East Coast, who bought the undeveloped land along the corridor between Los Angeles and Santa Barbara and started planting sugar beets, strawberries, and other crops.

Acre by acre, they eventually sold off their ranches and farms, and with two U.S. Navy bases located nearby after World War II—Point Mugu and Port Hueneme—the first wave of sailors and Japanese families moved in, followed by a second wave of Mexican migrant workers.

To newcomers like my mother with little money, Oxnard offered something they couldn't find in big cities: affordable mortgages, a slower pace, friendly people, simple values, a place where they could realistically rebuild her lives and put down roots.

When Marshall left after a few days, Mom rented a motel room for thirty-seven dollars a week. Left alone, she was unsure whether she had the strength to make it on the outside. But that flicker of a once-bright light, nearly extinguished by heavy medication and neglect, still burned in her. She checked the classified section of the *Oxnard Press-Courier* everyday for secretarial jobs and rooms to rent. Her secretarial skills had become rusty, so she practiced shorthand while listening to the words of radio commentators, and she took the bus downtown to practice on the library's typewriter. She couldn't afford to buy a car, even with the money from Daddy and Marshall.

When she had regained her skills, Mom applied for a job at the Kelly Girls temp agency and scored well enough on the tests to be sent on to a secretarial job the next day. She worked two temporary jobs for the next few months, and though she desperately wanted to see Kate and me, she wanted to wait until her circumstances improved. When she had enough savings, she bought a car and rented a room— with her own bath—in a woman's house near the center of town.

The woman was a Japanese immigrant, divorced, and she lived alone in a small three-bedroom tract house on a quiet street. She wanted to know where Mom had lived before, where she worked. Afraid the woman would reject her if she told the complete truth, Mom said she had been caring for her sick mother for the last several years in the San Fernando Valley, and now that her mother had passed away, she wanted to live in a smaller town. The woman agreed to take her in.

In those early days, alone and just starting out again, Mom's mind was often occupied with thoughts of seeing her daughters again. Any day now, she would be ready to invite us out for a visit, and then everything would be as it once was.

2 0

On Easter weekend in 1965, I nearly threw a tantrum when Daddy said we would be visiting Mom in Oxnard. "I'm not going and you can't make me!" I yelled. "Why do we have to go? We don't even know her anymore. I want to stay here with you."

"She's your mother and she's entitled to see you," he said firmly. "You're going and that's all there is to it."

Kate and I had seen Mom only once since that weekend of the pot roast explosion, and she had missed all the years in between. Kate didn't want to see her, either. We had adjusted to her long absence from our lives, and besides, we were now grown up—Kate seventeen, me fifteen. Sisters at the high school spoke of us as "young women," so we didn't need or want a mother anymore. That's what we told ourselves.

Now she expected us to pick up where we had left off, welcome her return and embrace her as our mother, as if the past had never happened. I cringe when I think about how insensitively I treated her when she got out of the hospital. I was young and wounded, and she was virtually a stranger—friends would tell me then to ease my conscience—but after all these years, I still cannot forgive myself.

Until Kate and I learned to drive and bought our own cars, the Greyhound bus was how we got to Oxnard. On our first trip that Easter weekend, Daddy drove us to the station on Vine Street in Hollywood and waited with us until our bus came, the one marked NORTH-SANTA BARBARA. On later trips he would just drop us off, wave good-bye, and drive away. His rush to leave made it seem as if he were glad to get rid of us, but in time I accepted his choice, realizing that our absence gave him a weekend of freedom when he could do as he pleased without any interference from us.

The bus station was a scary place. It had dirty floors, sticky in places from spilled soda and God knows what else, and the waiting room sometimes smelled of urine. There we were, two girls on our own, out of place among the winos, loners, and migrant workers. "What if some man tries to kidnap us?" I asked Daddy, hoping the idea might make him reconsider sending us on those trips.

"As soon as you open your mouth," he said with a playful smirk, "he'll run the other way."

"That's not funny," I scowled.

As the bus lumbered along the freeway, I gazed out the window at the passing cars, trying to keep count. The bus made at least seven stops before the driver announced, "Next stop, Oxnard." I looked for any signs that Mom was waiting for us, even while hoping she wouldn't come. I was afraid I wouldn't know how to act around her, afraid of what to say, of what she had become. What should I call her? All the normal endearments would be forced and artificial. The whole trip, in fact, seemed faked to me, and I was a fraud.

When the driver helped us off the bus. I kept looking down, hoping I wouldn't see her there. But then she came rushing toward us, her arms opened wide. She appeared old for her years, and her left eye drooped. When she smiled, I saw what the years of neglect had done to her teeth.

She took my face in her hands and kissed me. Unsure of how to respond, I called on my convent school manners. "How nice to see you," I said. "Thank you for coming to get us." Kate was even stiffer and pulled away when she tried to kiss her on the check. I could tell Mom felt awkward, too, but her discomfort came from a different source. In her depths of longing, she wanted to find a way back into our hearts and lives. We didn't make it easy for her to do that.

"I've got a nice weekend planned," she said as she carried our suitcases to her car. It was a used, faded-blue Ford Fairlane, and I remember thinking what a clunker it was compared to Daddy's classy Cadillac. I elbowed Kate to sit in the middle next to Mom, but she refused and climbed in the backseat.

As she drove, Mom kept on talking about the place she now called home. I stared out the window, thinking how unsophisticated everything around there seemed and how embarrassed I'd be if anyone I knew saw me riding in that old, run-down car in this cow town. Kate and I had no interest in how things were going for Mom, so we didn't ask her any questions about her life. We filtered everything through a judgmental lens, and for a long time there was nothing she could do right, certainly not like my father could.

I have little memory of the house where Mom lived in those early days, but I'll never forget her room. It was in back near the service porch, and there was only enough space for a double bed, a dresser, and a bookcase. I remember thinking how sad it was that a woman her age, ancient by my calculations, had so little, and I blamed her for her humble circumstances.

For Easter weekend, Mom had rented two cots and bought new sheets and blankets for us. She wanted everything to be perfect. When she offered to let Kate and me sleep in her double bed, we both groaned at the idea. We said something like "We'd rather die." She then suggested we take turns. Kate could have the bed Friday night, and I would sleep there Saturday. My sister declined and said Mom should sleep there. I considered the options between a big bed and those flimsy-looking cots. Kate glared at me and begrudgingly, against my better judgment, I also declined Mom's offer.

Much of that weekend is a blur except for Mom's eagerness to try to make us happy. We could have done almost anything—go to the beach, have dinner out, play miniature golf. The only requirement was attending Mass on Sunday, since Daddy had made Mom promise to take us. All I wanted to do was go home as soon as possible. Every day I pestered Mom to let me use her phone to keep in touch with him. He was the center of my world, and I didn't want him to be lonely without us.

"I miss you, Daddy," I would say on the phone. "Do you miss me?"

"Of course I do," he would say.

On Easter morning, when Kate and I woke up, Mom tiptoed around our cots and took two beautifully wrapped presents out of the closet. "Happy Easter, my little chickadees!" she said. "These are for you."

Kate unwrapped her gift carefully, trying not to tear the paper. I ripped mine off. Inside were our new Easter dresses. We laid them out on the bed. Kate's was purple, mine green. "Green is our color," Mom said to me. "It shows off our red hair." Kate and I stared at her. The dress sizes were for girls half our ages. "Go ahead, try them on," Mom said. "I'm hoping they fit well enough so you can wear them to church this morning."

"I'd have to be a baby to fit into this," I said, oblivious to the meaning of her mistake. Mom looked at us, then the dresses, and finally realized what the sizes meant.

"I guess I still think of you as my little girls," she said in an anguished voice.

But for us, what she said was too little, too late.

Six months later Mom got her first full-time job in the secretarial pool at Port Hueneme High School and finally made enough money to rent her own apartment. In applying for the job, she filled out several forms on her background and work experience. Dr. Goodman had told her that no one needed to know the details of her life, but as much as she feared that the truth might disqualify her for the job, she wrote down that she'd been a patient in Camarillo. When the principal asked her why she had been sent to a mental hospital, she answered, "I was in great emotional distress after my mother died and my husband divorced me." He hired her the same day.

Mom's workday consisted mostly of typing and filing, but she loved her job and took great pride in it. She liked the students and teachers breezing in and out of the administration office all day, asking questions, looking for files. All around her there was so much life, and she felt needed.

After a lot of practice, her typing and shorthand picked up speed, and she was often praised for being "the fastest secretary in the pool"—a trivial distinction to Kate and me. At first she thought she wouldn't fit in. Most of the other secretaries were younger women with husbands and children, and she worried they would find out about her past. The principal tried to reassure her. "It's nobody's business," he said. "Just do a good job; that's the important thing."

Mom tried to make friends by remembering her coworkers birthdays with cards, cakes, and baked cookies. At first they stopped by her desk to pick up the goodies, but in time they would stop just to talk to her.

When we visited at her apartment, she would talk about how happy she was at the school. She had begun socializing with new friends outside of work. One woman, a secretary about her age known as the school gossip, didn't like her. Kate and I thought she was probably jealous of Mom's popularity, but we didn't tell her our suspicions. One day during lunch hour, when everyone had left the administration office, the woman rifled through the staff's personnel records, found Mom's file, and saw she'd been a patient at Camarillo.

Mom couldn't figure out why some colleagues suddenly steered away from her as if she had chicken pox or some other disease. Her rival continued to spread the gossip, and finally it circled back to Mom. "I couldn't hold my head up anymore," she told us. As much as she loved her job, she resigned two weeks later.

The outcome hurt her deeply, and she feared her past was like a criminal record that would hold her back the rest of her life. Even after she was hired as a secretary at the Point Mugu naval base a few months later, she still talked about her life at the high school. Kate and I offered her no comfort. Whenever she talked about the past, about my father, their failed marriage, how she didn't belong at Camarillo, we cut her off in midsentence, rolled our eyes in exasperation, and changed the subject.

*   *   *

Over the next few years our visits with Mom became more regular, once every month or so in Oxnard or Los Angeles. But we continued to resist her efforts to reestablish a relationship with us, believing it was too late to recapture what had been lost so long ago.

I didn't tell her about the upcoming mother-daughter teas at Immaculate Heart High School so I could attend them with Mrs. Cavanaugh instead. Back then I was embarrassed to have my friends meet her. Mom had always longed to be a part of such events and would have been devastated over being excluded. At my high-school graduation, we seniors walked down the aisles of the Hollywood Bowl in long white gowns and carrying red roses. Kate and Daddy sat together in the box seats. Mom sat by herself in the side section. When she came backstage, I tried to usher her out quickly so my friends wouldn't see her—her synthetic dress, her skin marred by webs of red lines. My friends' mothers were around the same age, but to me they looked younger and more respectable in their expensive suits and coats from Bullock's and Saks Fifth Avenue.

When she drove to Los Angeles to see us, her old Fairlane would sputter and lurch on the Grapevine, the one-mile uphill grade on the 101 Freeway. Sometimes her car would break down in the far right lane. As she waited for the tow truck, steam poured out of the hood, but she was also concerned that the treats she had made for us—peach cobbler (my favorite dessert) or cheesecake—might get ruined in the hot sun.

To make extra money, Mom put on her straw hat and picked strawberries on the weekends for $2.75 an hour. Growers advertised for extra help during the harvest season, and in June and July the sun would bear down on fields filled with the old and young—whites, Mexicans, Japanese.

"You'd never catch me doing that," I said, embarrassed that she would stoop to do such menial work. However, I wasn't above enjoying the fruits of her labor. She made strawberry pie and shortcake with thick whipped cream, and she always saved a few boxes of plump strawberries for us to take home with us.

As the years passed and we spent more time with Mom, I felt myself softening toward her. She rarely criticized us. She might ask me, "What in the heck do you have on, dear?" when I wore my baggy flight suit or long skirt with the fringe, but that's about it. For no reason at all, she freely told us she loved us and continually gave to us. We were on the receiving end of things we'd never had before, all the things I never knew parents did for their children. She took us to the beach for picnics, to movies, to miniature golf, to department stores so we could pick out some new outfit. She let Kate date, wear makeup, and lie out by the pool in her two-piece bathing suit. Daddy had forbidden her to wear one like that because it was "much to risqué."

When we visited her apartment, I felt as if I were on vacation. She let us stay up late and sleep in, and we didn't have to do the dishes. "I want you girls to relax and have a good time," she would say. She made popcorn and kept me company as we watched my favorite TV horror show—*Chiller Theatre*—on Saturday nights. One of her nicknames for me was Honey Dear, two endearments in one. She bought me books, mysteries mostly, and knowing I liked animals, she gave me a Chia Pet, a toy sheep, as a Christmas present. I delighted in bringing its hard clay body to life, soaking it in water, planting grass seeds in the grooves of its chest and legs, watching in fascination as it sprouted a new green coat a week later.

One Easter she gave me a baby chick in a box. It was my first real pet since Peppy the turtle, and I kept it near the heater vent in my bedroom. The older it got, the messier it became. It would poop while standing in its food bowl, on the carpet, on top of my bed, anywhere. And I couldn't really bond with the chick. When Daddy said it was time to give him away, I felt sad but also relieved.

"Stop trying to buy us," I once told Mom when she gave me a new gadget. "I'm not trying to buy you," she said, surprised and indignant. "I do these things because I want to."

We were both right. She was trying to find a way back into our hearts in any way she could. And she also loved giving to us.

Sometimes on Sunday mornings she would quietly pull back the covers and crawl into bed next to me. I would pretend to be asleep as she gently stroked my hair away from my face, as she had done when I was a little girl. I wasn't used to such care, and it somehow repelled me. My wires were still crossed when it came to love, and if it came easily, as it did with Mom, I didn't trust it. Pretending to be groggy with sleep, I pushed her out of bed.

A few weeks before Christmas or Thanksgiving, we knew she would phone us. She would ask to spend the holiday with us, but for a long time we would answer, "Thanks, but we already have plans with Daddy." She thought he was pressuring us and tried to get him to be fair, pointing out that he had us over for the previous holiday, so now it was her turn.

"I don't understand why Gordon is so selfish," she would say about Daddy. She never hesitated to talk about him and revisit the past; she had been a good wife and mother and had never belonged at Camarillo. "I never wanted to leave you girls," she would say.

Then I always thought to myself: *If you loved us so much, why did you leave us?* But I never said it out loud.

For years I remained my father's staunch defender and cut Mom off when she brought him up. Around and around she went, again and again, the same stories from the past, as if repeating them would get rid of painful memories. Sometimes we became downright rude and would get up from the couch or kitchen table and walk away.

One Friday night after dinner, Mom got a phone call and started crying. Her best friend, Trudy Honald, whom she'd known for more than thirty years, had died from a heart attack the night before. Mom couldn't stop crying. When she seemed to be reaching the threshold of a complete breakdown, Kate turned cold and impatient.

"If you don't stop and get a hold of yourself," she said, "we're going to leave." Her harsh words startled me and I wanted to intervene, to try to convince her that our mother's grief was normal. But I said nothing. I just stood there watching Mom suffer.

"That's it," Kate said. "Mary, get you're things. We're going."

And so we left Mom, all alone, and drove back to Los Angeles. Nearly forty years later I still shudder when I think about what we did.

22

When I visited Mom over the years, I would often ask her to drive down Oxnard Boulevard so I could see if the black man was still standing by the side of the road, waving his white napkin. He worked for the Colonial House, Oxnard's best restaurant in the fifties and sixties, and its brochure would later refer to him as "unique advertising." People driving by couldn't miss seeing that big, burly man with round, bulky muscles and skin the color of a black eggplant, which made his white chef's uniform and tall, billowy hat stand out all the more.

On weekends and holidays he would stand for eight hours each day across the street from the restaurant, near the railroad tracks, on a raised wooden platform and wave his linen napkin at passing cars. His face glistened with sweat in hot weather, and his full lips were cracked. No matter what time of day it was, or how long he had been standing there, he would smile at passersby and keep waving his napkin. It seemed he took great pride in his job. But how could he? I wondered. He had a subservient, degrading job, and he allowed his blackness and racial history to be exploited. What did his family, his children, think about their father making such a spectacle of himself?

Something about him fascinated me. We had nothing in common, yet I felt a connection with him. At the time I wasn't sure what it was. Mom said that her Redheaded Missile—her latest nickname for me—was just being her usual inquisitive self, but my fixation with him went deeper than mere curiosity. I felt great respect for him and wanted to understand how he felt about being so exposed, how he could stand there with such dignity and openness, even when drivers honked at him or gave him the finger. He never wavered. He would just keep smiling and waving the napkin.

I first saw him in 1968 when I was sixteen. Earlier that year, in my history class, I had studied the Civil War era, so I knew something about slavery. At times I thought I was reading horror stories. How could whites treat black people in such gruesome, horrific ways? I remember pictures of slaves standing on platforms, in chains, being auctioned off to plantation owners. Children torn from their mothers, entire families split apart.

Before then, I had little awareness of civil rights. I grew up in a small box of middle-class life where I knew no blacks, and they were rarely mentioned in my home. Most whites were oblivious to the plight of black people and other minorities. My friends and I—and our families—were cocooned in our own lives, going to Mass on Sunday, praying that God would make us more loving and compassionate. Yet we remained unmoved by the reality of racial injustice.

When I read that Lincoln freed the slaves and the North won the war, somehow I thought the cruelty and injustice of slavery ended forever. Then, a few months later, I met Violet, the Cavanaugh's new maid, a lean, wiry young black woman who wore a crisp white uniform and soft white shoes. I watched Violet, busy in the kitchen, preparing our meal. When we were seated at the table, she served us individually, then put the serving dishes back in the kitchen. I watched her intently. She made a plate for herself, poured a glass of milk, set it on a tray, and carried it into the small room off the dining room—"the maid's room"—and closed the door.

The whole scene fascinated and perplexed me. It seemed odd that this woman who had done all the marketing, had cooked the meal and served it, and would likely clean up after us wouldn't share in it with us.

"Why is she eating in there and not with us?" I asked Mrs. Cavanaugh. My question hung in the hair for several moments without an answer.

"Well, because she works for us, and that's how these things are," Mr. Cavanaugh said. "Now eat your dinner before it gets cold."

And then a while later I saw the black man outside the Colonial House. Even after the restaurant closed down in the seventies, the image of him stayed in my mind. When we drove past the platform where he used to stand, I would stare out my window, my nose pressed against the glass, wondering what had become of him and worrying about myself—what I'd do with my life after I graduated from college, unaware that my interest in these displays of injustice would somehow develop into something more concrete.

Other than the Beatles and my friendships, nothing really moved me. I didn't feel passionate about anything. Maybe my long red hair would open up a career in TV shampoo commercials, my mother would say. Maybe, but that didn't feel right.

"Don't worry, dear," she would say, trying to comfort me. "You'll know when the time comes."

"But how will I know?" I said, trying to nail down specifics.

"One day you'll know. You just will."

23

From the time I was nineteen until I turned twenty-four, getting in trouble was the only thing that seemed to come naturally to me. Freed from the shackles of school and home, I looked to the outside world, pulsating with hope and change, for my rehabilitation. My behavior soon fit the classic story of a repressed Catholic girl gone wild, and like so many others in the sixties generation, I let my hair grow long, experimented with psychedelic drugs and sex, and fell in love with the Beatles.

I also began stealing.

My thieving had actually begun two years before, when I was seventeen, in a most daring way. After I got my learner's permit, I stole, of all things, my father's beloved green Cadillac. I didn't really steal it; I borrowed it one night after he was asleep and picked up my friend Sue Liberti, and we drove in the hills around Mulholland Drive. What a wonderful time we had, the top down, our hair blowing in the crisp night air, the radio blaring, laughing at our good fortune to be out, alone, on such a beautiful night. As I came around a curve, a little too fast, a sheriff's deputy saw me and pulled us over.

My father was going to be livid, I knew, so I came up with a plan. In the morning, knowing that at any moment the deputy would call my father to report my caper, I fell on his mercy and confessed my crime. "I know how wrong I was," I said, contritely. "I know how foolish and dangerous it was. I only hope you can forgive me. I'll never, ever do it again."

After the deputy called, my father said he was considering sending me away to a reform school, but he never did.

Two years later I stole again when I visited Berkeley, California. Back then the town almost begged you to break the law and defy the establishment. It was the center of student radicalism, the hotbed of protest against the Vietnam War, the police, parents, and authority of all kinds.

My friend Elaine, a freshman at UC-Berkeley, invited me for a visit, but I was ambivalent about going. I was afraid I'd get snared in some protest march and be exposed as a political lightweight. Put on the spot about my opinions, I could talk authoritatively about the Beatles all day long—and could sing the lyrics to most of their songs—but beyond believing that the war was wrong, I possessed only the dimmest understanding of the politics behind it. Kate made me feel less apathetic when she said, "We've got our own internal struggles to worry about."

On Saturday, Elaine and I strolled down Telegraph Avenue, the main street in Berkeley, which in those days was a carnival of the counterculture. The sidewalks were barely passable, crowded with young people dressed in faded jeans, colorful long skirts, some in bare feet, most with long hair, some to their waists. They sat on corners and outside coffeehouses, playing guitars, their dogs sitting at their feet, with no leashes on. There were dogs everywhere, it seemed, and they roamed free, another symbol of the liberated times.

I couldn't believe how many people kissed right on the street where everyone could see them. I blushed when I passed by kissing couples, both admiring their openness and feeling how repressed I was by comparison. I wasn't a complete prude. I had kissed a few boys and had sex with one, but seeing as how it hurt and I bled, sex wasn't something I wanted to repeat anytime soon.

MAKE LOVE, NOT WAR stickers were plastered on store windows, on schoolbooks, on car bumpers. The smell of patchouli oil and incense coated the air and swirled through my head, all of the sights, sounds, and smells intoxicating my senses with a feeling of freedom, of potential and change.

On Sunday morning, still groggy and in a crabby mood as usual, Elaine peered into her refrigerator. "Damn it," she said. "There's nothing to eat." She said it as if it were an aberration, not its chronic state. Elaine lived with two roommates, and a quick survey of our group revealed that we had, in total, about twenty dollars, not enough to go out to breakfast.

So we decided to head over to the nearest market. It was gray and overcast outside and looked as if it might rain. Elaine lent me one of her coats, which was warm enough but much too big for me. We didn't have an official plan, but it was understood that each of us would be responsible for stealing something for our breakfast and dinner.

Inside the market we split up and went in different directions. I headed for the meat counter, where I spotted a huge honey-baked ham wrapped in clear cellophane. Without question, a superb contribution. But I froze. I moved on to the chicken section, but it didn't hold the same allure. Looking around to see if any employees were watching, I walked back, unbuttoned Elaine's coat, took a deep breath, and grabbed the ham. It was heavier than I expected, and I struggled to tuck it under my left arm. I strolled down the aisles just like any other casual shopper. A woman gave me a strange look, and I could see why. With my left side ballooning out, I appeared horribly deformed.

Buoyed by my newly exercised boldness, I took a half-gallon carton of fresh orange juice and tucked it under my right arm, so now, though still uneven, my chest was not nearly as conspicuous. Before leaving the store, I glanced at the magazine rack, as if I had all the time in the world, and then I casually walked out the side door. Except for cruising the hills in my father's Cadillac, I had never felt so free and alive.

Elaine and I met up around the corner. She had a pack of cheddar cheese and a carton of eggs in her big black purse, and a bottle of red wine inside her coat. But when I laid out my ham on the kitchen table at the apartment, her roommates cheered the loudest.

A few months later I stole some makeup at a Sav-On drugstore near my apartment in Los Angeles. I worked part time for an interior decorator then while I attended UCLA, and she had taken me under her wing to give me "feminine" guidance.

I had quit the phone company a few months before, when I turned twenty-one, out of shame more than boredom, and I knew the managers were glad to see me go. One had marked in my personnel file that she thought I might be "unstable." One day I had come in exhausted and disoriented, partly from smoking grass the night before, partly from my chronic malaise, but most directly from the car accident I'd been in the previous week. Another vehicle had plowed into the back of my car, leaving me with a stiff neck that was giving me headaches. After an hour on the job, everything imploded. I felt dizzy and started breathing rapidly. My supervisor had me lie down in the Quiet Room and called paramedics and my father. He got there in time to see me carried out on a stretcher.

In the emergency room a doctor found nothing wrong with me physically, so he prescribed a muscle relaxer and had me breathe through an oxygen mask for several minutes. My father stood next to me, holding my hand. I knew what he was thinking—just like my mother, another step closer to the inevitable end—and I wondered if he might be right.

A few months later another incident occurred. I lived then with my friend Kathy, who also worked at the phone company, and we shared a small, one-bedroom apartment in the Hollywood Hills. When I came home in the evenings, I would often find bloodstained cotton balls and used syringes tossed in the bushes by neighborhood junkies.

One day I was home alone—Kathy was at her boyfriend's apartment—and I followed my usual routine: dinner, then reading on the couch, gazing out the window, wondering when my life would finally begin in earnest and I could start being happy. On the way to the kitchen to wash the dishes, I picked up a razor blade from the bathroom cabinet. As I stood over the kitchen sink, I paused to consider if I really wanted to do this. I used the razor to make superficial cuts on the inside of my left arm. But then I decided that I didn't really want to hurt myself; I just wanted to feel someway other than the way I felt.

I wiped off the few spots of blood, stared out the window, and with complete resignation called, of all people, my father. I told him about everything: my loneliness, the drugs, my disappointing sexual encounters with boys, my fears of not measuring up, of not knowing where I was headed in life.

He didn't scold or criticize me. He just listened. It was as if he had known that the time would come and he would now fulfill his preordained role again. As he had with Mom, he would now take his daughter to a psychiatric hospital. He picked me up and drove to

UCLA's Neuropsychiatric Institute. We filled out the forms and waited in the lobby. Two psychiatrists eventually interviewed me. They asked about my appetite and diet, how well I slept, and what books I liked to read. Part of me wanted them to believe I was emotionally troubled, to get attention, so I told them my favorite books were *The Stranger* and *The Bell Jar.* They scribbled that down in their notebooks.

Back in the lobby, my father and I barely spoke. Doctors dressed in white coats, nurses carrying clipboards breezed by us, all looking very serious. The minute hand was broken on the large round clock on the wall opposite us, and I found it odd that no one had bothered to fix it. A few patients dressed in hospital gowns walked by with attendants guiding them. It was a world unto itself—clean, sterile, gray walls, busy with people coming and going, none of them looking very happy.

One of the psychiatrists eventually joined us. "We'd like to keep her here for a few days for observation," he said, talking to my father as if I weren't there. "We'll be able to tell more then." I gave my father our "evil eye" look—our code frown that meant we wanted to escape whatever was happening.

Outside, I breathed in the fresh, clear air, animated by all the life I saw around me. And then I knew. I knew this was not my destiny after all. "Let's get out of here, Daddy," I said. "I don't belong here. Take me home."

And he did.

My new job with the interior decorator was a relief from the phone company. I typed only a few invoices a day; the rest of the time I talked to her vendors and clients on the phone. In those days motherly advice came so rarely that I grabbed onto her feminine guidance as if it were the Gospel. At her house she gave me a makeover, applying blue and gray shades of eyeliner, brown-black mascara, and peach blush. "With your fair skin," she said, "you must wear a liquid foundation. It's necessary if you want to look your best."

I was nearly broke, but she convinced me that getting the makeup was an essential step in becoming an attractive woman. So I went to a Savon drugstore and, one by one, slipped the recommended items in my purse. As I walked out of the store toward the parking lot, I exhaled, feeling relieved that again I had not gotten caught. Then I heard footsteps behind me and felt a hand on my shoulder. "Come with me, miss," the store detective said.

Mortified, I walked back into the store, where employees glared at me. In a private room, the detective told me to open my purse. The mascara and bottle of liquid foundation tumbled out. He looked at my license, and seeing that I was only nineteen, he said he would call my parents instead of the police. I begged him not to contact my father. Better the police than him. I knew Daddy would show me no mercy, and even though I wasn't technically a minor, I feared he would send me away to some reform school, as he had threatened to do before.

I broke down sobbing. Maybe because I looked sweet and innocent, or maybe because he was just a nice guy, to my amazement he let me go with only a warning.

"For your sake, young lady," he said, "there better not be a next time."

I swore to myself it would never happen again. Much too risky. But the beautiful red-and-gold Oriental rug in the foyer of an apartment building on Wilton Avenue was a whole other situation and put me back in business. It was actually Kevin Sanborn's idea to steal it, but I didn't need much coaxing to be his accomplice. Kevin was the first man I loved, and in 1972 when I was twenty-one, without telling my father, we moved in together in a cozy one-bedroom apartment that had been part of Charlie Chaplin's old film studio in Hollywood.

Kevin's mother used to say of her son, "He's the most perfect of all my children." I knew what she meant. He was gentle, smart, generous, and good looking, but he hung around with a crowd of junkies and thieves. I knew them, too. One stole my purse when he saw it lying on my bed.

In targeting the rug, Kevin and I rationalized that our place, while cozy and fully furnished, lacked items of quality. Late one night we parked across the street from the apartment building and entered the foyer. Up close, we saw it was a fake Oriental rug, which soothed my conscience. We rolled it up, carried it away on our shoulders like construction workers with a heavy beam, and shoved it in the backseat of my blue VW. As we were driving off, a car pulled up behind us. We prayed that the people in the other car had not noticed us. But they had. They wrote down my license plate number and called the police.

Two days later there was a knock at my front door. Surprise. It was my father. I suspected he was there about the rug—the VW was registered in both our names, and the police had called him—but a far greater fear made my heart pound. I worried that he would discover I was living with a man. He had always threatened to disown Kate and me if he ever found out we were "living in sin."

I let him in, then excused myself to use the bathroom. Frantically I hid all traces of Kevin's presence—his aftershave lotion, razor, shirts, underwear, and sports jackets all went under the bed. I returned to the front room.

"I'm going to ask you straight out," Daddy said. "Look me in the eye and tell me the truth. Did you steal that rug?"

"No, Daddy, I didn't. I swear it."

"Then you won't mind going to the police station and answering a few questions. They'll give you a polygraph if they think you're not telling the truth."

My mind raced. What should I do? I called a lawyer I had worked for the previous summer. "Did you do it?" he asked. "Never mind. I don't want to know. The important thing is that you *not* submit to a lie detector test. They can't force you. Just tell them that you refuse the test on the advice of your attorney."

For the police interview I wore the most innocent Catholic-looking outfit I had—a gray pleated skirt, long-sleeved, white button-up shirt, and navy-blue cardigan sweater—and I pulled my hair back in a ponytail and tied it with a pink ribbon. No one could possibly suspect me, I thought.

The detective grilled me for an hour about my activities the day of the theft. I thought I did exceptionally well in answering his questions, but when it was over, he said, "I don't believe a word you're saying. I want you to take a polygraph now."

I panicked for an instant, but then composed myself, looked him straight in the eye, and replied, "No, officer. On the advice of my attorney, I won't be doing that."

Late one night a few days later, Kevin and I used another car to return the rug to the foyer. With no evidence, the case against me went away.

Again I was lucky, but I knew I was teetering on the edge of disaster. I would have to get rid of my criminal tendencies and buckle down to the business of living a respectable life.

24

With working part time, it took me until I was twenty-seven to graduate from UCLA, but even then I still floundered, without a clue of where I was headed. I considered psychiatric social work, thinking I knew more than most about the mentally ill and could be their Dr. Goodman. I volunteered at a psychiatric halfway house, but that didn't last even a full day. Much too depressing. Then I decided I wanted to go out in the world of ideas, where I could create something of great value. I took out an ad in a media magazine with the headline I HAVE A BRAIN AND WON'T SETTLE FOR ANYTHING LESS THAN THE CHANCE TO USE IT.

"Dear Brain," one response began, and I ended up taking that job offer at a PR firm. But I left after a month because the boss couldn't meet payroll.

The only thing I really loved was jazz dancing. I took lessons at Steven Peck's dance studio and deluded myself into thinking that at twenty-eight I still might have a chance to dance professionally. It was the first endeavor, other than stealing, that made me feel alive and capable. At first I felt foolish and klutzy as I strutted across the dance floor, my hips gyrating to sensual Latin music. I got good enough, or so I thought, to go on to a few auditions, but when I never made the final cut, I knew it was time to try something else. But what?

Dancing provided me with a general clue: I yearned to step out of my small self, my limited life, and find a way to express myself. But how? I did know that my current job as an assistant at an ad agency wasn't the answer. My boss asked me daily to get his coffee and sharpen his pencils. I did it a few times until one day I couldn't keep quiet anymore. "You know, Dan," I said politely, "the pencil sharpener and coffee room are as close to your office as they are to my desk. It just seems logical that you could go yourself."

Had he not been such a nice man, he might have thrown me out then, but I limped along for another few months, desperate to find my niche.

On the way to work one day in the summer of 1978, I saw a billboard announcing the publication of a new magazine: NEW WEST, A MAGAZINE FOR CALIFORNIA. It intrigued me. Next to dancing, I loved books and magazines, and for years I had harbored a persistent but vague notion that I wanted to be a writer. In my college years I worked part time at the *Pico Post,* a small community newspaper, hoping to get my start that way. I rewrote press releases about upcoming golf tournaments and charity luncheons, becoming so restless I thought I'd jump out of my chair. I longed to sink my teeth into something interesting and important.

One day I received a tip about a slum landlord who was cheating his tenants over their rental checks. I asked my editor to let me pursue the story, but she said it wasn't in the "purview" of my job. A few days later my friend Debbie, lowering her voice to sound like my mother, called the editor and said that I had suddenly come down with hepatitis and wouldn't be returning.

My favorite magazine was the *Atlantic Monthly*. I loved those pages dense with words, hardly any photographs, and I would run my hand over the glossy pages, trying to absorb the words into my body. Here were people doing what I wanted to do: expressing their thoughts and opinions about things that mattered.

I sent my résumé to *New West,* and when I didn't get a response, I headed over there one evening after work. The office was still under construction and had working phones but no desks. The managing editor said she liked my "initiative" and recommended me for an editorial-assistant position. During my interview with one of the editors, a man I'll call Dave, he took a black-and-white photo out of his in-box and showed it to me—an erect penis sticking up through a phone dial. He laughed uproariously and watched for my reaction. I smiled faintly, thought he was an idiot, and kept my mouth shut.

He was the first of several such editors I would work with over the years. Back then, displays of vulgarity didn't matter much. I could take the sexual innuendos, the low pay—$750 a month—and the long hours, because I had found my way into an exciting new world of ideas and writing.

Two weeks after my thirtieth birthday, I gave up my cozy guesthouse in Beverly Hills, sold my VW, and gave my furniture away. With two suitcases and my Royal typewriter, I took the red-eye on a rainy April Fools' night to New York to become a real writer. With only three magazine articles to my credit, I was a lightweight but "aspiring" writer, and I yearned to stir souls the way mine had been when I read Carson McCullers' *The Heart Is a Lonely Hunter* and William Styron's *Lie Down in Darkness.* At the very least, I wanted to accelerate my career in magazines.

In between my secretarial and fact-checking duties at *New West,*

I had written three articles: an arts piece about the San Francisco Ballet, a consumer-alert story about the toxic additives in ice cream, and a first-person essay about the tyranny of nonsmokers, titled "Pains in the Ash." I still smoked cigarettes then and was annoyed by the righteousness of those who treated me like a leper.

Nothing I had written even remotely approached brilliant prose, but at least I had been published and figured that now, with barely those three clips, I'd be able to find a writing job in New York.

The day before I left, Mom drove down from Oxnard to say good-bye. She wanted to take me out to dinner, but I already had plans with my father. She brought an assortment of gifts, including a gray wool neck muffler with matching gloves and a leather-bound journal. "This is what writers do," she said, handing me the journal. "Who knows, maybe one day you'll write a book." Then she gave me a sweet good-bye card with a $250 check inside. "I just can't believe it," she said, crying. "My little girl is leaving."

That night Daddy told me to "dress up really nice." He would take me to Perino's, the restaurant in Los Angeles where the city's elite dined. I dressed in my black crepe pants, a black blouse, and low black heels. When I got in his Cadillac, he looked at me and said, "What have you got on? I told you to wear something nice." The evening had only just begun and already he had managed to devastate me. I could have dressed in a black dress, but on that night, nothing I wore would have satisfied him. Deep down he found unacceptable what couldn't be changed: I was leaving him.

Midway through our meal, after he'd had two martinis, I asked, "So what do you think about my going to New York?" I hoped he would say something along the lines of what Mom had told me— she was proud of me, it took courage to head off to a new world, I was smart and clever and could do anything I set my mind to.

"Here's what I think," he said as he lit another cigarette. "I think you're a fool going to a fool's city. Your place is here. I'll give you a thousand dollars if you stay, but nothing if you go." A big part of me didn't want to leave. I was frightened about going to New York alone, with no job, no place to live, but I also knew that I *had* to leave if I was ever to break free of the past and find my own way in the world.

As it was, I kept being drawn into the quicksand of what was familiar: attracted to men like my father, charming, good-looking men, but hopelessly crippled emotionally and unavailable for a serious relationship. It still astonishes me what I made do with back then. I had affairs with men who stood me up, men who said they would call after we had slept together but never did, married men who came to my house for dinner and sex and then left a few hours later and returned to their wives.

In a way it would have been easy to go on offering up my life for his. It's what I was used to. Pleasing him was like a powerful current that swelled with hope and then was dashed at each bend in the long, unending river of sadness that flowed into my dreams.

I wasn't aware of the deeper meaning of my unhappiness. I had lived that way for so long, believing that longing and loneliness were just a way of life. Yet something inside, a faint voice, maybe the same flicker of light that had guided my mother, made me think there had to be something better.

I might not have been strong enough to pull away from the past had it not been for the dream I had a few weeks after I started therapy. In it, I was riding in a car with my father. He was at the wheel, in control as usual, looking straight ahead at the road. I looked over at him and studied his profile for a long time, seeing both the father I loved and the man who kept hurting me. In the dream I picked up the gun in my lap, pressed it against my father's right temple, and pulled the trigger. He fell into my lap, his blood mixing with my tears. When I began caressing his face, my anger vanished and I tried desperately to revive him. But it was too late.

I woke up sweating, and for weeks I couldn't shake the horror of that dream. At times I felt dazed and ill, as if I were under some kind of spell, and at other times the meaning of the dream was unmistakable to me—my father had to die so I could live.

Now, on that rainy night when I headed off to a new life, I was leaving the people I loved, instead of them leaving me. But it hurt just as bad.

25

I could tell you many stories about the four years I lived in New York—wild, weird, wonderful tales—but it would take another book to cover that experience in any detail. New York was the Ph.D. of my life. It wrung from me every ounce of my will and strength, and in return it gave me a stronger belief in who and what I am. Awed by the city's splendor, I felt as if I had moved to the center of the universe, as if I were one of life's chosen, when I walked down Fifth Avenue.

On the downside, I would tell you how I, a California native, suffered in the dense, wet heat of summer and, worse, the bitter cold of winter, when I would struggle against the fierce winds, slip on icy sidewalks, and then stand hunched over, my toes so cold I was sure I had hypothermia, while waiting for a bus. My mother, worried about how I was faring, sent me an electric blanket.

On the bright side, I would tell of a generous friend, Arlene Aizer, whom I'd first met at *New West* magazine. She invited me to stay with her in the apartment of her parents on the East Side while I looked for my own place. The clean, spacious apartment gave me the notion that I could readily find an apartment just as nice.

However, I soon discovered that competition for even dismal apartments raged through the city, and some were barely bigger than the closets in California homes. Cockroaches, bold and fearless, didn't bother scurrying away when the tenant turned on the lights.

I would tell stories about moving my belongings in the backseats of cabs from sublet to sublet until, after seven months, I found a small rent-controlled apartment of my own. When I applied, the manager said he would put me at the top of his long waiting list if I would let him visit me in my apartment from time to time. I smiled sweetly, offered him a box of chocolates instead, and moved in.

There would be the stories about men in subways and on sidewalks who waited until I made eye contact with them before unzipping their pants and masturbating—in public. Stories about men I fell in love with—for one magical night—as we walked down Park Avenue, hand in hand, the white Christmas lights twinkling in the trees. The story about the first man who gave me an orgasm, after which he said he had nothing else to offer me.

And I would tell of my first Christmas there, alone, except for an hour with strangers in a church, listening to the angelic choir. I heard people say that it took two years to make a new life in most cities and twice as long in New York. I often thought of moving back home. I never knew how much I loved California until I left it.

My father eventually sent me the thousand dollars with a note that made me cry: *"My dear Mary: Hang on, Honey. I know you can do it. P.S. Don't tell Joanne I sent you this money."* Despite his view of New York as a "fool's city," I think he would have visited me if he had not undergone quadruple bypass surgery. Kate promised to visit, but she never did. She was always too busy. My good friend Liz came out in the fall of 1982, followed by my mother the following spring. For Mom it was a trip down memory lane. She had fond memories of "Ol' New York," the city of her youth, where she had danced at Red Cross benefits and lunched with her own mother at the Russian Tea Room.

A couple of times, when Mom and I walked past the Plaza Hotel and strolled through Central Park, she began looking wistful, as if she were thinking back on what her life might have been like if she had not married my father and taken a different road.

In the beginning, I took any freelance assignment I could get. I thought the three story clippings I had brought with me from *New West* would open doors, but I might as well have shown editors blank pieces of paper. Finally, the *Village Voice* hired me to write about the Dance Theatre of Harlem. I managed to get a cab to take me uptown past 125th Street, but after my interview with Arthur Mitchell, the troupe's founder, I couldn't find a cab back for the life of me. When black men in cars slowed down and offered me rides, I remembered Mom's warning when I left Los Angeles: "Don't go into an elevator or anywhere else, alone, with a strange man." After waiting about an hour, I finally realized that cab drivers didn't want to search for passengers in Harlem. So I took the bus.

Once I wrote a story for *Rolling Stone* about the Polish novelist Jerzy Kozinski, whose new novel, *Being There,* had just been made into a movie. An intense man, he had dark, beady eyes that seemed to bore through me. He shared his Park Avenue apartment with Kiki, his longtime partner, and wrote a moving dedication to her in his book: "To Kiki, for showing me that love is more than the longing to be together."

A few days after the interview, Kozinski called me around midnight and began telling me about the sexual habits of Americans versus Europeans. I figured he was trying to get chummy to in-fluence how I wrote the story, but what a strange, off-the-wall subject to discuss with a reporter. Years later I read that he had killed himself. The report said he pulled a plastic bag over his head and died in his study, the room where I had interviewed him.

Other assignments followed, including two short-lived staff ed-itor jobs. One resulted in my first press junket—an unforgettable week of wine tasting in Rome and Florence sponsored by the House of Ruffino. Things were looking up. I had many more published credits now and had accomplished what I had set out to do—accel-erate my journalism career—but I still felt undirected, without pas-sion for anything I wrote, and I kept missing my true home. So I moved back to Los Angeles.

From the day the McMartin preschool molestation story broke on February 2, 1984, in Los Angeles, the media were major players in the story. I remember the frenzy in Wayne Satz's voice when he reported the allegations on KABC-TV that night: "More than sixty children, some of them as young as two years of age . . . who were enrolled in the McMartin preschool in Manhattan Beach, have now each told au-thorities that he or she had been keeping a grotesque secret of being sexually abused and made to appear in pornographic films while in the preschool's care—and of having been forced to witness the muti-lation and killing of animals to scare kids into staying silent."

That story set off the panic.

The bizarre, incredible allegations took off like wildfire. Like most people there—and soon the entire country—I was glued to my TV set as members of the McMartin family and other teachers at the preschool were arrested, put in shackles, and sent off to jail to await trial.

Of course they're guilty, most people said. "Where there's smoke, there's fire." And I agreed. They must be guilty. Otherwise, how did all these allegations come about?

A week later I was sitting in *People* magazine's conference room with several other reporters, feeling bored and restless, as the bureau chief divvied up the week's assignments. One was about Elizabeth Taylor's recent admittance to a Santa Monica hospital for her addiction to painkillers, another was the breaking news story about the McMartin case. I had gone to work for *People* as a freelancer when I returned from New York, and for the first few months I was content to float from one lightweight assignment to the next, unmoved and uninspired by most of them, unaware that something more was possible.

I wrote "trend" stories about men who wore ponytails and women who pierced their noses and belly buttons, "split" stories about celebrities getting divorced, and "sequel" stories about what had become of performers like Nanette Fabray and the Disney Mouseketeers.

At the *People* meeting, the bureau chief instructed us to "throw out the net" on the Elizabeth Taylor story, which meant interviewing as many people as possible who had any connection, however remote, to her: her hairdresser, her hairdresser's hairdresser, her dog groomer, her masseuse, her facialist. I rolled my eyes at a colleague sitting across the table. It all seemed so ridiculous. The bureau chief caught my look and gave me the unenviable task of interviewing as many of her ex-husbands as possible. I thought about the reality of the assignment for a moment—the awkwardness and utter invasiveness of it—and with an alacrity and flash of defiance that surprised even me, replied, "You've *got* to be kidding!"

The room fell silent. In the world of celebrity journalism, most of us had had those thoughts from time to time but never dared express them. We were regularly reminded that there were a hundred other reporters dying to take our place, and had I not found a way to quickly redeem myself, imminent termination probably would have been my fate.

Since no one wanted to go to Manhattan Beach that weekend and report on the McMartin case, I volunteered.

26

I first met Kate's dog, Charlie, during one of my visits from New York. A terrier mix with fluffy white hair, he was napping on my sister's couch, a sliver of the afternoon sun casting a triangle of light on his back. I thought he was cute, but I didn't pay much attention to him. It's not that I didn't like dogs. I did. I just wasn't noticing them much anymore because I was busy pursuing my career. The part of me that once cared for another living being had faded away.

Charlie had been a stray. A friend of Kate's had found him wandering in the hills around the Greek Theatre in Hollywood. Skinny, his hair dirty and matted, he was wary of strangers but sweet and gentle when they showed him kindness. She took him home, but since she already had four dogs, she passed Charlie on to Kate.

It was a happy, creative time in Kate's life, except for the blow from my father when she told him she had moved in with her boyfriend, Carl. "I love him, Daddy," she said, bracing for his reaction, "and we're very happy. Please be happy for me."

"You're nothing but a whore," he told her.

And with that, she hung up on him and they did not speak again for five years.

I pretended to like Carl but thought he was full of himself. He smoked a pipe, wore tweed jackets, and, à la Ernest Hemingway, hung a stuffed moose head in the bathroom. Kate had started seeing him a year earlier when he was still married. His wife became suspicious he was having an affair when he began spending more evenings "at work." That led to their separation and divorce.

Kate treated Carl like a king. He liked to eat, so she pored over cookbooks and prepared extravagant meals: crown roasts, alternating the tips with cherry tomatoes and white miniature chef's hats; prime rib au jus; potatoes au gratin; pâté; pineapple cake—all for a man she yearned to please.

When they moved in together, she sought ideas for decoration in design magazines, shopped for colorful fabrics to reupholster the couch, and revived her sewing skills from her days at Ramona Convent. She made throw pillows, curtains for the kitchen and bathroom, and velvet dresses—one dark forest green, the other burgundy—for Carl's two little girls. When they stayed every other weekend, Kate treated them the way she had longed to be treated when she was their age. She took them to dance performances and movies, played children's games with them, and taught them how to sew clothes for their dolls.

When I saw them all together, I was struck by the uncanny replica of our own family history—a single father, a girlfriend, and his two little daughters. Carl even looked and talked like Daddy. He would say his favorite line over and over, and always with a playful smirk: "My problem, Mary, is that I've been misunderstood by women all my life." The links to Daddy escaped Kate as she basked in the comfort of feeling loved and being a part of a family.

One day, after they had been living together for two years, Kate emptied the pockets in his sports jackets to take them to the dry cleaner and found a credit card receipt from a Holiday Inn. Her suspicions aroused, she rifled through his drawers and found receipts for jewelry and flowers. She fell in a heap on the floor, sobbing. When Carl came home, she confronted him, but he denied he was having an affair with his blond assistant at work, claiming that he was just helping her through a divorce.

"A leopard doesn't change its spots," a friend told Kate. "My God," Kate said one day as the connection to her past gripped her. "I fell in love with a man just like my father."

Devastated, she moved out, took Charlie, and got her own apartment. For months she was inconsolable. I remember her talking on the phone with her friend Lynn, crying, sipping a glass of red wine, trying to ease her grief. One warm, sunny afternoon, as she rehashed the details with Lynn, she forgot to turn the heater off and her apartment sweltered. Lost in her pain, she seemed oblivious to her surroundings. The condition of her carpets escaped her, as did the growing flea population on Charlie. When I walked on the rug in her bedroom, a cuff of the black insects immediately circled my ankles.

My sister seemed to be at the same juncture of loss and grief that our mother had gone through all those years ago. I wanted to console her, but I didn't know how. I called Mom, put Charlie in my rental car, and drove to Oxnard to spend the rest of the weekend with her. Together we washed Charlie on the patio and combed out the fleas. For dinner, she made him hamburger, and at night he slept with me on the pullout couch.

When I moved back from New York, Kate and I lived together. We had been roommates before, in our twenties, but with mixed results. Our first apartment was a studio, and we slept in the living room on twin beds that rolled halfway under a side table and turned into truncated couches during the day.

The setting didn't work out for long. A few times I walked in on Kate having sex with her boyfriend, a nice guy named Darrell, who was the best man at my father's wedding with Joanne. Or I would stumble in around two or three in the morning, usually stoned, and wake her up. It was the early seventies, and I brought home an odd assortment of people, hippies and druggies, so they could crash on our floor. In the dark, seeing only their long hair, Kate couldn't tell if they were male or female. "Who was that?" she would say in the morning.

A few months later we moved into a one-bedroom apartment in Hollywood, just down the street from a bar that stayed opened twenty-four hours a day. We split all the bills, but we bought our own groceries. Kate had the left side of the refrigerator, which was always full of appealing items like orange juice, pie, and ice cream. When I went to the market, I usually had only enough money for basics. If I asked my sister for a piece of pie, she would always say, "No, get your own." Her unrelenting stinginess resurrected my thieving impulse.

When she left, I poured half a glass of orange juice and put in tap water to bring the container back to its original level. I took slivers of her cheese and boysenberry pies, but was never greedy. I only took tiny slices so she wouldn't notice anything missing. Once I asked to borrow a quarter to do my laundry. "Use your own money," she said.

"Come on," I said. "It's only a quarter." But she wouldn't budge.

By then, I'd had it. My temper rose like a rocket. I grabbed a small paring knife and threw it at the wall near where she was standing. It missed her by several feet and fell to the floor. I never meant to hit her, but the damage was done. She didn't trust me after that, and even less when I took her car a few weeks later. Mine was in a shop for repairs, and I wanted to meet a friend at a movie theater.

After Kate fell asleep, I took her keys and quietly inched her brown Ford out of the driveway. I was back by midnight, but it wasn't soon enough. She was waiting for me, fuming so much that I thought I could see smoke streaming out of her ears. I knew it was wrong to take her car without permission, but somehow I felt justified.

A few weeks later we moved out and went our separate ways.

By the time I returned from New York in 1983, our resentments had faded and I joined Kate and her new boyfriend, Steven, along with Charlie, in the house she had bought in the mountains above downtown Los Angeles. On the first night, Kate told me not to eat dinner because she was making me a special "Welcome home, Mary" dinner. I was touched by her thoughtfulness and felt that now things would be different between us. It was a grand night. I hit it off with her new boyfriend, we made each other laugh, and after a tasty feast of Indian food and generous servings of red wine, he and I acted out skits from TV's *I Love Lucy,* only he put on a scarf and played Lucy and I played Ethel.

When I walked into the kitchen in the morning, I found a grocery receipt on the counter. It showed the total—about sixty dollars—for the previous night's dinner, circled in Kate's handwriting and the cost divided by three. Along the side, she wrote, "Mary, you owe $20." There it was again; I had been home for less than a day, and there was another example of her stinginess. I sank into old dark places, thinking that things would never be different from the past. No spontaneous giving, no helping each other out unless it was paid for right down to the penny. On Christmas that year she bought a roll of film for six dollars and whispered in my ear, "You owe me three dollars."

Other than work—freelance assignments for *People* magazine— and paying $275 a month in rent, I had no responsibilities and lived like a teenager. I breezed in and out of Kate's house with little thought of anything outside my own existence. I couldn't cook any- thing besides broiled chicken and scrambled eggs and, except for a framed reproduction of Monet's *Water Lilies,* the walls in my bed- room were bare.

Kate was the adult. She owned the house, and on weekends she made repairs and worked in the garden. I watched her plant a cac- tus garden on the side of the house that got full sun, but for a long time their beauty escaped me. I saw only ugly prickles.

About the only thing I had strong feelings about was running: It was my passion. I ran five miles, five days a week, on the college track near the house, or at the beach on weekends when the tide was low. As I ran, drenched in glorious sweat, I would feel I was being transported to another world of pure elation and clarity.

During that time, I began to connect with Charlie. In those ear- lier years, I would just pat his head when he greeted me at the door, and sometimes I would take him for a little walk when Kate came home late. Other than that, I pretty much ignored him. He was Kate's dog, Kate's responsibility.

One evening we came home around the same time and saw a brown pile on the white living room carpet next to the sliding glass door. Charlie had been sick the day before and had obviously come down with the runs. Kate threw a fit. She dragged Charlie by his collar until he was standing over the runny mess. "Bad dog!" she yelled. "Bad dog!" Then she whacked him on the backside and pushed his head down toward the pile until his nose grazed it. Charlie whimpered, ran away, and hid in Kate's closet the rest of the night.

I was sorry for the poor dog but glad that it hadn't happened on my carpet so I wasn't responsible to clean up the foul mess. But something stayed with me; something about it felt familiar, and later that night I made the connection as memories came flooding back—my father beating our dog Queenie in the garage, me standing in the door, a silent witness, aching to do something but doing nothing. The parallels to our past came clear as if someone had suddenly turned the light on in a darkroom.

Charlie was innocent. The poor thing got sick, and Kate had not provided him with a way to get out of the house on his own. Apparently he had tried. He made his mess right near the sliding glass door that led out to the deck. If it was anyone's fault, I thought, it was Kate's.

After that, I began to pay attention to how she treated Charlie. I knew she loved him; she called him "Sweet Pea" and let him sleep with her. But her love was the kind we had known growing up, and she ignored all but his most basic needs. She walked him five minutes in the morning, five at night, but there were no hikes, no walks in the park, and no playing ball with him. She fed him in the evening, but he left much of the food, a reddish-brown slop, in the bowl and eventually developed skin rashes.

When his ears became infected, a common condition with terriers, Kate would see him shaking his head in obvious discomfort, but she didn't take him to the vet for days. She was too busy. One morning I heard a car's brakes screech, and when I looked out the living-room window, I saw Charlie cowering in the middle of the street. The car had barely missed him. A few weeks later he wandered off again, apparently a habit of male dogs who haven't been fixed. We searched in all his regular hiding places but found no sign of him. "Here, Charlie," we kept calling.

"Well, that's it," Kate said when it got dark. "He's gone." She went back in the house and closed the door. He was gone and that was that.

I continued looking for him the next morning. As I walked by a neighbor's yard, I looked through the fence slats and saw something moving. It was Charlie, trying to hump the neighbor's poodle.

I was surprised at how happy I was to see him again. My worries vanished, my whole body relaxed.

27

Everyone cried at Mom's wedding in 1981—even the minister, who hardly knew her. We gathered in a lovely garden in back of a Presbyterian church in Oxnard. Those of us in the small group who knew my mother's history cried because we understood the significance of that day. We knew how far she had come, and now, after so much loss and sadness, at the age of seventy-one, she had found love again. People who didn't know much about her past life cried because there was something so hopeful about the ceremony. Even late in life, there was still the chance of falling in love.

Mom looked radiant that day, better than I had ever seen her. She wore a kelly-green silk dress and a corsage of gardenias. She could hear us sniffling behind her as she said her vows, but she did not cry. The struggles and miseries of the past were finally over; she had crossed the river and now stood on firm dry ground on the other side.

In the years after Camarillo, Mom had one disappointing dating experience after another, and Kate and I found her stories amusing. A friend set her up with a man from Texas who took her to dinner at the Whale's Tail in the harbor. When he parked the car and got out, Mom waited inside, thinking he was going around to open her door. A few moments passed, but the man didn't come. When she looked up again, she saw him standing at the restaurant's front door, waving at her to join him.

"Well, I never," she told us later. "What's this world coming to when a man can't even open the door for a lady?" Another man who "seemed nice enough," Mom said, "expected me to go to bed with him on the second date. Imagine that!"

In the end, she married Harold Hanson, a kind, simple man whose greatest pleasures were camping and eating. He loved to eat because he never got enough as a child. He was born in Norway, the eldest of twelve children in a poor family, and he never made it past the seventh grade because he had to quit school and help support his eleven brothers and sisters. When I knew him, he looked like an aging John Wayne, still hardy, with strong, tanned thighs from riding his bicycle all over town. He was hard of hearing and often got things mixed up. If someone asked him when the pie would be ready, he would say something like "No, sorry, we don't have any rye bread." On Easter one year, we were discussing how fast Oxnard was growing, and he responded, "We tried growing rosebushes but there just wasn't enough sun."

"Oh, Hal, pay attention," Mom would say. She sometimes doubted that she should marry him, thinking he was beneath her because of his limited education. But he was a good man and he loved her. Seeing her reflection in a shop window one day, Hal said, "You sure do have a lot of mileage on you, but to me you're still the most beautiful woman I've ever seen." She had loved my father more, but she had learned the hard way to look beyond the charm and the surface of a man.

They had a good life together. They rode bikes and picnicked on the beach, and Hal barbecued on the patio of their condominium.

He liked to take Mom camping, cook hamburgers on a grill, drink beer, play his guitar under the stars, and finish off the evening by having sex with Mom in the back of his VW van.

"Frankly," she told me one day, covering her mouth with her hand to muffle the heresy she was about to confess, "I could do without sex altogether. Hal would have sex every night and morning if I'd let him." Mom wasn't crazy about camping, either. She had to be cramped in the van's small space, and mosquitoes a mile away would find her, as they always did me.

As the years passed, the center of our family gradually shifted away from Daddy toward Mom. She no longer had to beg us to visit her; we went without being asked. I felt completely at ease there, as if a cage door had opened and I was now free to be myself without fear of being punished.

"This is your home, too," she would say. "Come as often as you like, and bring Charlie." I liked and admired the person she had become, and I no longer felt that I had to hide her from my friends. Kate and I started bringing a few of them, along with Charlie, for the weekend or just for the day. We would sit out by the pool as Hal marinated steaks and cooked them on the grill. Mom made margaritas and baked mushrooms, our favorite appetizer.

To surprise her, I checked the classifieds in the Oxnard newspaper for a used piano. I found one, an upright, and bargained with the owners and got them to bring the price down by a hundred dollars, to five hundred. Mom was thrilled. Now she could play again. She and Hal paid cash for it and moved it to their condominium in his VW van.

Holidays were no longer a source of conflict. We split them: Mom's place on Christmas Day and Easter Sunday, and Daddy and

Joanne's apartment on Christmas Eve. Mom took pride in decorating her dining-room table with colorful tablecloths and matching napkins, centerpieces of Easter baskets with colored eggs, small holly wreaths and poinsettias at Christmas. She always had her camera nearby and took endless photos of us. The past was gone, and she wanted to document the present to make sure it was real.

In the box of old photos I found a year ago in my basement, I found pictures of us—our new family of five: Mom, Hal, Kate, and me, and Charlie in my lap.

A few months after Joanne married Daddy, she got a rude awakening when a credit card company was attached to her bank account. Daddy owed about a thousand dollars on his American Express card, and once the newlyweds had a joint account, creditors came after her. When they were dating, Daddy had never let on that he was in financial straits, and he paid for their dinners with his card. He was working hard in his real estate business and thought he was about to sell a bank and the landmark Wiltern Theatre. But the sellers backed out at the last minute.

As the market slumped, so did Daddy's health, and he stopped working, at the age of fifty-eight. Joanne supported them on her phone company salary. Golf became his new passion. He went all out and wore madras pants, alligator logo shirts, and white buck shoes, and he drove to the golf course nearly every day. His other passion was for a Boston terrier named Brandy, short for Gordon's Spot o' Brandy. He became devoted to the puppy, walked him regularly, and played with him on the carpet, getting down on his knees and hugging him and speaking in a gentle voice. Kate and I had never seen him so attached to anyone, human or animal.

On Joanne's birthday in 1984, we went out to dinner at Lawry's restaurant, which was famous for its prime rib. We were standing in the crowded bar, having a drink, when my father collapsed on the floor. Kate and I thought he was having a heart attack. The bartender called the paramedics, but Daddy refused to go to the hospital. "I'll be all right," he said. "Just take me home." He started popping nitroglycerin pills as if they were breath mints, and any day when he had to walk upstairs or carry anything heavier than a briefcase, he would put several under his tongue.

A few months later he had a mild stroke. "No fried foods and no cigarettes!" his doctor ordered. "This is serious, Gordon. You can't keep smoking and expect to live." Daddy tried to quit but started up again a week later.

"Oh, you know how your father is," Joanne said when I worried. "He doesn't like being told what to do."

I once thought that his stubbornness was part of what made him strong, part of why I looked up to him and tried to emulate him. But now all of that seemed foolish and childish to me, and for the first time I saw the depths of his inner compulsion to self-destruct.

A few months later he had another stroke. When I visited him in the hospital, his mouth was open and a remote control lay near his right hand. He had only sparse, gray hair around his temples and deep, puffy folds circled his eyes. As I studied his face, I tried to remember the handsome man who dressed in dark silk suits, the man who had had such power over me. It surprised me that seeing him so old and frail didn't make me love him less, as I had thought it would. I had been taught, by him, that love was based on the external—on youth, physical beauty, expensive clothes, financial success, where someone lived, what car they drove, and, most of all, on being invulnerable. And yet here he was, weak and frightened, his good looks and fierceness gone but his essence still intact, and my love for him remained steadfast.

When he woke up and looked at me with sad, searching eyes, I leaned over and kissed his cheek. He turned away so I wouldn't see him cry. "It's OK," I said. "You'll come through this just fine." I had seen him cry once, maybe twice, but now he looked at me, imploring like a helpless child. Wasn't there something his younger and most devoted daughter could do to save him from this fate? I buried my head in his chest, my tears washing over the scar from his open-heart surgery the previous year, a narrow gulley that ran from the base of his throat all the way to the middle of his stomach.

He never regained his health. Doctors cut into his brain to implant a spaghetti-like tube that drained the fluids causing his disorientation. But that didn't help restore his memories. When I showed him a picture of a chair or our old house, he didn't know what they were. And he had forgotten the name of his first wife, the one in Hawaii, and my mother's name. Did the past matter anymore if he couldn't remember any of it?

His dog, Brandy, was the only thing that stirred a reaction in him. "I swear he loves that dog more than he ever loved us," Kate said. After he was released from the hospital, Daddy asked out of the blue to see Kate. We were stunned. They had not seen or spoken to each other in five years, not since he had called Kate a whore after she moved in with her boyfriend.

"Maybe it's worth a shot," I said, urging Kate to visit him. "He's not going to live much longer." When we went to his apartment, he smiled and hugged her. They tried to make small talk. Finally Kate asked to speak with him in private in his den.

When they came out twenty minutes later, I saw tears in my father's eyes. "Come on, Mary," Kate said. "It's time to go."

Later she told me what she had said to him in trying to rid herself of the feelings that had festered in her for many years. "You treat your dog better than you ever treated us," she said. "We were your children, and all you gave us was food, shelter, and clothing. You were selfish and cruel. You caused so much pain in our lives and Mom's life."

She said he bowed his head as tears filled his eyes. Then he looked up at her and said, in a faint, childlike voice, what I had never heard from him—"I'm sorry."

That was the last time Kate ever saw him. She refused to see him in his final days, saying she had already buried him. By then, I had undergone several years of therapy and come to see that my father had probably done his best, given the limits of how he was raised and difficulties in his own life, and that like all of us, he had struggled to find a way in which he could experience some measure of happiness before his time was up.

I visited him in the convalescent home a few days before he died. His eyes wandered and he didn't seem to recognize me, but I like to think he knew I was sitting there on the edge of his bed, holding his hand, and that he heard me say that I forgave him for everything and would always love him.

As he wished, he was cremated and his ashes were scattered over the ocean. There was no memorial service. No one except my stepmother and me would have attended. He had no friends anymore, and he had not kept up with his relatives in Ohio.

I needed to find some way to say farewell and honor his leaving this earth. So I wrote him a poem, then lit a match to the paper and wrapped the ashes in a piece of tinfoil. Early one morning, I drove alone to the beach near the Santa Monica Pier and walked through the cold sand to the shoreline.

I gazed out at the gray, choppy ocean and whispered good-bye to my father, now floating out there in the vast waters.

As a wave circled my feet, I opened the tinfoil and let the wave take the ashes out to him.

28

Kate and I weren't prepared for how bad Mom looked when we visited her on Easter Sunday in 1985. Two years before, she had been diagnosed with uterine cancer, but with surgery and chemotherapy it had gone into remission. Now it was back. Still, her spirits remained optimistic. "I'm going to beat this thing," she would say, and we believed her. Until we saw her that day. She had lost more than twenty pounds and her hair was thinning, but she had gone all out as usual in preparing for our visit.

The table was decorated with fresh-cut flowers and a basket filled with colored eggs, and she had dressed in a yellow organza dress—she even had on pantyhose. When we were seated around the dining table, Hal served the ham, but Mom ate only a few bites. Seeing our tears, she said, "Don't be sad, girls. It's a part of life."

After lunch she sat down at the piano and played like old times, her fingers dancing gracefully over the keys, half singing, half humming the lyrics. She knew she was dying, yet she didn't show any fear. Weak and emaciated, her thin neck swimming in the collar of her dress, her voice faint, she never looked more beautiful and at peace as she began the last song, "The Impossible

Dream," its lyrics of unbearable sorrow and righting the unrightable wrong, no matter how hopeless, seared into our hearts. She sang of her life, its tragedy and triumph, going, as the song said, where the brave don't go, to fight with her last ounce of courage, even when scorned and covered with scars, to reach, as she did, the unreachable star.

Kate and I ran to the bedroom, sobbing. Later that day, as Mom rested on her bed, I lay down across from her. "You know, dear," she said, "your only problem is that you don't know your own worth. If you could only see what I see." Knowing her time was running out, she added her next most important piece of advice. "And don't be alone," she said. "Life is hard enough without being all alone. Find a good man who respects you, one who loves you a little more than you love him."

Through my tears, I finally told her of my shame and regret for having treated her so callously in the years after her release from Camarillo. "Can you forgive me?" I said.

Smiling, reaching her hand toward mine, she said, "There's no need, honey. I understand why you were that way."

Late one evening in September, the call came from her doctor. "She's terminal," he said. When his words sank in, the blood drained from my face and I felt a horrible chilling effect as all the dread and inescapable finality closed around me.

Hal met Kate and me at the hospital. Mom shared a room with a woman who was also dying of cancer. We closed the curtain for privacy. I stood beside her bed, watching life fading from her thin, cancer-ravaged body. I couldn't bear to lose her again, and I crawled into the bed and lay beside her. We didn't need words to appreciate the significance of that moment, that we had finally come full circle, and as I held her frail hand, in my desperation I made her promise that she would find a way to connect with me from the other side and let me know she was all right.

"I promise," she said, "if there's a way, I'll find it." Then her hand slipped from my grasp, and she drifted off into a morphine sleep. Kate and I took a short break for dinner. When we returned thirty minutes later, she was gone. Her connection to us was so strong that she could only let go when we weren't around her.

Before Mom died I used to think along traditional lines about what people could inherit—if you were lucky, you got tangible things like jewelry, stocks, and insurance policies. But Mom left behind none of that. Just her example of how one human being, with her goodness and strength of character (like that potato in the jar of water), could find her way out of all that darkness and rediscover what she had always believed—that the real things of value reside in the domain of the human heart. Mom demonstrated what a parent, what a person, could be and left behind a legacy of love that guided Kate and me from then on.

Mom had asked to be cremated and her ashes buried next to her mother's grave in a cemetery in the Valley, near where we used to live. When I went to the front office to retrieve her ashes, the man at the desk returned with a box wrapped in brown paper. To my horror, it was still warm. All that was left of my mom, like my father, was a small box of her ashes, still warm from the flames. I thought I would never be able to accept death—hers, mine, all death—unless I could make sense of it. Did it mean my mother was extinct now, and that no trace of her, not even her soul or consciousness, remained? Or did the soul live on in a better place, as I prayed it did? What was the point of life, anyway?

Many of Mom's friends and former coworkers came to the memorial at her condominium. It was so crowded, some had to stand outside in the front yard. Hal, my mother's dear Hal, often cried as he passed around appetizers and filled the glasses of guests. As I mingled through the crowd, I was struck by how differently the lives of my mother and father had ended, one surrounded by so much love, the other with a single poem washed out to sea. When I noticed people looking at me intently, I knew they were thinking how much I resembled my mother. I smiled at them, proud to be Mom's daughter.

For months, sunk deep in grief, I waited and watched for that sign from Mom. But none came. Then I had the dream. In it I was hurrying to get dressed for some important event as my mother stood near the front door. When I was about to leave, she handed me a little purse. *Here, honey, take this with you.* I thought it odd she would give me a purse when she could see I already had one, but when I took it I saw how extraordinary it was, small and delicate and intricately embroidered with tiny jewels. It was too small to put anything inside, except maybe lipstick and a set of keys, but its usefulness lay in its exquisite beauty.

Then, in the morning, it dawned on me. The purse was the sign she had promised to send. It was as if her spirit was in the purse, because from then on I woke up to the world around me. And I felt the stirrings of a greater potential, a feeling there was something deeper, something more that I could do or contribute that would have meaning.

part three Criminal

Charlie, Scout, and me in 1991.

29

It was around this time that I embarked on my secret life as a dognapper and began to believe that the McMartin defendants had been falsely accused.

A few months after Mom died, Kate gave Charlie to an animal shelter. The demands of her ten-hour-a-day job as a telemarketing manager became overwhelming, and the grueling two-hour round-trip commute to Orange County left her with little energy. When she got home, she usually skipped dinner and drank a few glasses of white wine to unwind. If I was around before she got home, I would walk Charlie up the street, but other than that, it didn't occur to me to help out with his care.

It was a good time for my sister and me. We became closer after our parents died and lived together peacefully, yet we were still bound by our wounds from the past, and also stuck because of them. Our early life had taught us that we were on our own and should not look to anyone, including each other, for help. So we remained two islands unto ourselves.

The woman who ran the animal shelter promised to try to find Charlie a new home, but there was no guarantee, she said. He might have to be put down. I did nothing for two days, thinking that fate would take its course, but then something clicked in me, and I drove to the shelter and brought Charlie back home.

In looking after him the way she had, I don't think Kate knew there was any other way—it had been the same for her, and she was just repeating the pattern. However, I was tired of the old way, tired of the emotional crumbs, the deprivation, the emptiness, and from then on I got more involved with Charlie's care and grew to love him.

For the first time I noticed what a wonderful being he was, a true individual with many facets to his personality. He could be incredibly stubborn and sometimes growl to let me know he had limits on how I could treat him—especially if I took away a treat before he was done with it. At other times, he was gentle and gracious, like a real gentleman, prompting my friend Jenna to call him a "little man."

I enjoyed his company, and we took long walks at the beach and on the trails in the mountains near the house. I trained him to go down the hill into the park at the foot of Kate's house so he could roam freely until I whistled for him to come back. Then he would sit in the driveway, soaking up the morning sun.

I began feeding him a better brand of food and sometimes added chicken and rice. I loved watching him eat, taking in nourishment I had provided. When Kate and I were both gone, I left Charlie outside in the front, tied on a long rope, so he could see the world passing by. I arranged with our next-door neighbor to put him back in the house after a couple of hours.

After Charlie had hip surgery, I sat with him outside in the sun. "You sure do love that dog," Kate said. "You would make a good mother." I was stunned. No one had ever said anything like that to me. The prospect of being a mother, of having a family, was a remote idea to me. Families were for other people, and I looked on marriage and motherhood as one might a hole in the head: Why would anyone want to do such a thing? To me, marriage and motherhood were synonymous with tragedy and sorrowful endings, and I steered clear of both.

I decided it was time to live on my own and moved out in the summer of 1988 and bought my own house, less than a mile away, a charming green-and-dark-purple Craftsman house on a hill with a view of the San Gabriel Mountains. It had a yard and garden, which meant I could bring Charlie over. Kate and I reached an agreement: We would share custody of him.

I didn't think I would ever become attached to a dog again, but there I was, missing him terribly on the days Kate had him. If she was at work, she kept him in her house all day. I couldn't get the image of him, locked up and alone, out of my mind; it stirred old feelings from my years at Ramona Convent. It didn't make sense. Why would Kate keep him locked up in her house for ten hours a day when he could play in my yard and be with me as I wrote my freelance articles? Then it dawned on me: This was about unearthed relics of rivalries and resentments from our past.

One day a neighbor of Kate's called me. "I thought you should know," he said. "Charlie is lying in the middle of the street and your sister isn't home."

I immediately drove to her house and sure enough, there he was, lying in the sun in the street. I took him home with me. Kate explained that when he didn't respond to her whistle and

stayed in the park longer than she could wait for him, she had left
for work.

In my mind her priorities were mixed up. How could she
just leave Charlie, not knowing if he would run off or get hit by
a car?

I longed to have Charlie full time and began to fear for his
safety. I fantasized about stealing him but knew that it could end my
relationship with the only remaining member of my family. Yet I
loved Charlie, and he made me happy. After agonizing over what I
should do, I discussed it with my psychologist, Dr. Janos Kalla, a
warm, wise man who knew my past. Ordinarily he never weighed
in with his personal opinion, but this time he didn't hesitate. "Dake
da dog," he said in his Hungarian accent.

I installed a dog door and prepared my yard, fixing all the holes
in the fence, and had Charlie's file recorded in my name in the vet's
office. When I knew he would be secure at my house, I met Kate for
lunch.

"I'd like your blessing to have Charlie full time," I said. "I have
a yard, and he's almost never alone."

"No, he's my dog. You can't have him."

"Well, then, I'm taking him."

And so I did.

For a week after I took Charlie, we lived like fugitives, barricaded
inside my house with all the doors locked in case Kate tried to
snatch him back. I also kept the front gate at the bottom of my steps
locked at all times to prevent anyone from entering my property.

Kate was furious and called the police. An officer from the Department of Animal Regulation came to my house, but he couldn't

get beyond the locked gate. So he left a notice: THE DEPARTMENT HAS REASON TO BELIEVE YOU ARE HOUSING AN UNLICENSED ANIMAL. I panicked. Kate would show proof of her ownership, and I might be arrested. But it turned out that she had never licensed Charlie with the city, so I drove downtown with Charlie in the passenger seat and registered him in my name.

Kate told her friends that I had stolen her dog. "Maybe she needs him," one friend theorized. I could understand Kate's fury, but I figured that someday she would understand that the origins of my thieving impulse went back to our common experiences in childhood and that I finally came of age in middle age, by taking Charlie.

After two weeks with no break-ins, I relaxed and began a normal life with Charlie. His temperament was just what I needed. He was a gentle dog who eagerly accepted all the love I showed him— and he returned the feelings. He slept on my bed, nestled in the curve of my legs, and when I worked on a story, he would curl up on a rug under my desk. Sometimes I wrote for eight hours or more, and he would just wait patiently, taking naps until I got up and gave myself a break.

Then I would take him outside in the garden and direct his attention to the myriad of fragrant smells, the cool grass, the hummingbirds, the warmth of the sun, hoping he would stay outside. But as soon as I headed back inside the house, he would follow and stay close to my side. When I was outside gardening or reading, he would lie on the chaise longue, napping and soaking in the sun. When I unlocked the front door, he was always there, dancing excitedly, his tail wagging as if I had been away for weeks.

I loved Charlie's ears the best. When I pulled them up over his head, he looked as if he were wearing a World War II pilot's hat. When I put them under his chin, he looked as if he were wearing a bonnet. I had several nicknames for him: Charlie Pants, Sir Charles, and Lammer, because he looked part lamb.

I loved taking care of him, feeling responsible for a living being other than just myself. I particularly liked watching him eat. There was something so satisfying about providing him with nourishment that sustained his life. A new nurturing side of me emerged—one I didn't know I had. And I experienced love in the same way I had with my mother. Love became a constant; it didn't seem like it would leave, and I could love without fear of losing Charlie's love for me.

I took Charlie for walks at the college a few blocks away from my house. In the large grassy fields I removed his leash and let him run free. He rolled over in the cool, lush grass, all four paws dancing in the air, the picture of pure contentment.

I took him wherever it was allowed, and even some places where it wasn't. Like the bank and the video store.

On Christmas Eve, six months after I stole Charlie, Kate finally called me. "So, are we going to see each other on Christmas?" she said. Time and reason had changed her outlook, and I was impressed by her gracious acknowledgment that Charlie was "better off" with me.

I never thought I could love a dog more than I did Charlie. Then, a year later, I found Scout at the pound. She was a scraggly mess, her hair tangled and knotted, and she looked like a scrawny rat. She was a four-month-old schnauzer mix, with the most adorable face I'd ever seen. She, too, had been a stray and was picked up on a Pasadena street where she was scavenging for food near a Dumpster.

I wasn't sure I wanted another dog. What would be the effect on Charlie? Friends convinced me that a companion, especially an adorable little terrier, would be just right for him. So I took her in and never had any doubt about the name I would give her. Like millions of other girls who had read *To Kill a Mockingbird,* I had long ago fallen in love with Atticus Finch, the idealized father, and his sassy tomboy of a daughter, Scout.

Housebreaking her was nerve racking at times. I kept her barricaded in the kitchen, the floor covered in newspaper, but she hated being left alone and whined nonstop. "Don't give in to her," my boyfriend, Gary, said. "You have to be strong."

Thank God, Scout was smart, and it didn't take long for her to use the doggy door to go outside and relieve herself. She ate like a truck driver and soon put on a few needed pounds. Even though she was much younger than Charlie (he was about ten) and often got more attention from people when we went out for walks, Charlie never showed any jealousy. A model of dignity, he looked out for Scout as if she were his little sister.

At night I now had two lovely dogs sleeping on the bed with me, my new family, all of us warm and cozy. My favorite moments were sitting on the bed with them, watching the TV news and eating my dinner. Sometimes when they napped on the couch, I would tiptoe into the living room to watch them, feeling deep satisfaction that I was providing them with a good home and a full life.

When I drove them to the college for walks, both of them sat quietly, one in front of the other in the passenger seat, Scout fitting perfectly against Charlie's chest. Scout liked to run around in circles. She ran like lightning—first one way, then circling back and going the other way. Charlie and I tried to catch her, but she was too fast for us. She chased balls and sticks for a while, but then she got bored. When she was tired or didn't want to go on a certain route, she just stopped and refused to move. She always got her way.

When I took them to the beach, the waves frightened Scout at first. Terriers don't like water the way Labs do, so neither of them ever went in the surf. I would bring a book with me but usually never opened it. The dogs were so fascinating to watch as they ran free along the beach, chasing each other and nipping the other's legs. Their happiness made me happy.

On Thanksgiving that year, Kate invited all three of us to her house. It was one of the best holiday gatherings I can remember. Ten people. Our friends. Kate's fiancé. And Hal, Mom's widower. We gathered at the long dining-room table, laughing and toasting each other, and the memory of Mom. Charlie napped in his favorite chair near the sliding glass door while Scout, tuckered out from playing, slept at my feet under the table.

I wish I could say that the good times for Kate and me lasted, but they didn't. After she married in the early nineties and moved out of state, things between us deteriorated. When friends ask me what went wrong, I tell them it's a long story, not one specific thing. After Mom died, a new layer of resentment took hold as we unconsciously blamed each other for being all that was left. We had gotten used to her love, flourished with it, and once it was gone, we had to make do with crumbs again because we were unpracticed in knowing how to love each other. The Charlie incident didn't help; she trusted me less after that. On my end, I grew weary of her selfishness and obsession with money; it made me feel unloved. I remember calling her with the news that Charlie was failing. He was sixteen then and his back legs had given out. I was going to have him put to sleep the following Wednesday.

It was such a sad day. My friend Diana came with me to the vet's office, as did Scout. We all huddled in the exam room, and as I held Charlie on my lap, the vet put the needle in his right leg, and forty seconds later he was gone. We had a candlelight vigil for Charlie back at my house, and a few days later I scattered his ashes in his favorite spot at the park, near the waterfall. I found it strange that I never heard from Kate after I put Charlie to sleep. I thought she might call to see how I was doing.

I wrote her a letter in 1992 explaining the reasons why I needed to "take a step back for a while." I wrote that we had "different definitions of family," and I wanted something more now. I had hoped that Mom's example would guide us, but in the end, ghosts from the past came between us and I needed to flee from the old ways of being.

As the years passed and I never got a response from Kate to my letter, I often cried, thinking how sad it was that everyone in my family was gone now. Friends urged me to call her, but I couldn't. I was finally free of the past and was desperate not to return.

30

In reading the history of nations, we find that, like individuals, they have their whims and their peculiarities; their seasons of excitement and recklessness, when they care not what they do. We find that whole communities suddenly fix their minds on one object and go mad in its pursuit; that millions of people become simultaneously impressed with one delusion, and run after it, until their attention is caught by some new folly more captivating than the first.

— CHARLES MACKAY, 1841

The McMartin case was one of those once-, maybe twice-in-a-lifetime assignments, and it profoundly changed me and the way I viewed my profession. By the time I took the assignment, I had covered automaker John DeLorean's cocaine-trafficking case, along with other criminal trials, so I wasn't naive about how the criminal justice system worked. Most people are surprised to learn this—I know I was—but trials aren't about finding truth and justice; they are about winning. Prosecutors and defense lawyers employ perfectly legal methods to shade the truth and keep it from coming out, and bolster their positions by routinely spinning their side in the press. Accordingly, I filtered everything they told me through a skeptical lens. I subscribed to journalism's cardinal rule to be objective, to leave out emotion, and report the facts in a balanced way.

When I went to Manhattan Beach on that weekend on assignment for *People,* I kept those directives in mind as I interviewed as many people as I could find who knew the McMartins. The preschool had been started in the thirties by Virginia McMartin, a respected presence in the community. As she got older, she passed the school on to the next generation, Peggy McMartin Buckey, her daughter, and her grandchildren, Ray Buckey and Peggy Ann Buckey.

I went to their house first—it was next to the boardwalk—and knocked on the door, but no one answered. I was relieved. The thought of meeting these scary people made me nervous, but I needn't have worried. Except for Charles Buckey, Ray and Peggy Ann's father, the entire family—including seventy-two-year-old Virginia McMartin—was sitting in jail.

Next, I knocked on their neighbor's doors. One man said he thought twenty-four-year-old Ray Buckey, the chief defendant in the case, played volleyball on the beach too much. Another neighbor said she thought it was "odd" that she never saw Ray bring home any girls. I stood outside the church the family attended and interviewed their fellow parishioners. I interviewed people who lived on either side of the preschool on Manhattan Beach Boulevard, and except for those comments from the neighbors, no one had a bad word to say about the defendants.

Strange, I thought. *How can my reporting be so at odds with the other coverage that trumpeted the charges as fact? Maybe I missed something.*

When I returned to the bureau after that weekend, I wrote up my findings, concluding that "there was no there there," and sent the file to an editor in the New York office. When her rewrite came back to me, I was stunned. The editor had slanted the story to make the family appear guilty, although nothing in my reporting substantiated that. I argued with the editor, and her only defense was that everyone else in the media thought they were guilty, too. "But they haven't even gone on trial yet," I said.

A few days later the story hit the stands with the headline CALIFORNIA'S NIGHTMARE NURSERY. I felt angry and unsettled, betrayed even, and was spurred on to investigate the case more thoroughly.

When I discovered the facts of how the case came into being, I was stunned and thought that any day the authorities would recognize their mistake and let the defendants go free. And when they didn't, I discovered the real crimes were those of the prosecutors and the press, whose bad judgment and unrelenting bias ruined the lives and reputations of these defendants.

It began in late 1983 when a mentally disturbed woman, Judy Johnson, called Manhattan Beach detective Jane Hoag and said somebody called "Mr. Ray" had sodomized her preverbal two-and-a-half-year-old son at the nursery. (She later went on to accuse other men, including a U.S. Marine.) Officers investigated but couldn't find any evidence to support the charge. However, their suspicions extended to the possible abuse of other children in the preschool, and less than a month after Hoag received the first call, her captain wrote a letter to two hundred McMartin parents. It named Raymond Buckey, grandson of Virginia McMartin, as the prime suspect, and urged the parents to question and examine their children for any signs of being molested. After that, all objectivity was lost.

Pamphlets were also sent out stating, "First and foremost, if your children confide that they have been sexually assaulted, *believe them*." It also advised parents to be wary of possible abuse by babysitters, teachers, neighbors, relatives, and older children.

Politics then entered the case. Robert Philibosian, the Los Angeles district attorney facing a tough battle against Ira Reiner in a coming election, was persuaded by his advisers to focus the attention of voters on McMartin. Public outrage over child sex abuse, they said, would be his best shot against Reiner. He authorized Children's Institute International to begin questioning the preschool children.

Kee MacFarlane, an unlicensed social worker, led the interrogations of dozens of children. She had them play with puppets and dolls with oversized genitalia while she coaxed them into telling her about "yucky things" Ray Buckey, then in his early twenties, and other McMartin teachers might have done to them. Her interview methods eventually led to charges that more than three hundred children had been molested at the preschool over the past decade.

MacFarlane passed the results of her work on to Wayne Satz, the KABC-TV reporter who first broke the story and continued using her findings in his ongoing reports. As it would later come out during the trial, she and Satz soon became lovers and lived together.

Soon the public was flooded with stories of the defendants flying preschool children to Mexico, where men were waiting to sexually molest them. Other children said they were forced to dig up a grave in a cemetery next to a busy street (presumably in broad daylight, when they were supposed to be in school) and stand there looking down at the corpse while Buckey warned them that they would be buried, too, if they dared to tattle. Or, children said, they were taken down a storm tunnel (via a grille on the edge of a busy street) and led by Buckey to the shoreline of the Pacific Ocean, where more molesters were waiting. After a flight to a ranch north-east of Los Angeles, the kids said they were molested, then forced to watch the butchering of a horse and other animals as another warning not to tell their mothers about any bad things when they returned to the preschool after a two-hour adventure.

What in the world is going on? I thought. *How could these things have gone on for years with parents coming to and from the school at all hours of the day? It just doesn't make sense.*

Things got even stranger. Satanic cults became a major element in the McMartin case and at least a hundred others. Believers were thought to have been inspired by the movie *The Exorcist* and subsequent films on the same theme. One psychiatrist theorized that such cults arose from the testimony of multiple-personality women under hypnosis. They told their therapists of being captured and molested in childhood by devil worshippers, and then later repeated their stories at national conferences of child protection workers and law enforcement officials.

Then the "experts" moved in, and while they conceded that children readily make up all kinds of stories, they declared that *children never lie about sexual abuse.* Roland Summit, the psychiatrist who became a leading figure in the McMartin and similar cases, was among the first experts to declare and uphold the children-never-lie doctrine. In early stages of the McMartin case, Summit appeared frequently in the media to explain how the alleged horrors at the McMartin preschool could be understood in scientific terms, and he counseled parents and worked closely with investigators and prosecutors. He was credited (or blamed) for helping bring out a radically new concept: Everybody, man or woman, has an innate sexual lust for little children. Thus, he concluded, anybody can be drawn into "a battle between good and evil."

As panic spread across the country, his doctrine became the

driving force against the accused in the absence of credible evidence. And once accused, in the midst of such fevered hysteria, the person was presumed guilty until proven innocent.

Meanwhile, the McMartin defendants—Ray Buckey; his grandmother Virginia McMartin; his mother, Peggy McMartin Buckey; his sister, Peggy Ann; and three other teachers—were starting out on a rugged road in the criminal justice system.

I first met Ray Buckey in February 1988 in the county jail in downtown Los Angeles, where he was held under a three-million-dollar bail for five years. By then I had left *People* and was on assignment for *Life*. Except for Buckey and his mother, the charges against the other McMartin defendants had been dropped for lack of evidence. Charged with sixty-five counts of child molestation, including rape, sodomy, and oral copulation, Buckey, then twenty-nine, had lived in isolation in a concrete-encased ten-by-twelve-foot cell since his arrest in February 1984. Vilified in the press, I expected him to be dark and menacing.

As I passed through the security checks, and two motorized cell doors closed behind me, I had the strange feeling that I'd been here before. And in a way I had. I felt as if I were returning to Ramona Convent.

Buckey, his ankles shackled and wrists chained to his waist, walked toward me with short, hobbled steps. He was tall and gangling, and most of his teeth were brown stubs from grinding them at night. His skin was chalky and white, the pallor of a corpse; he had not been allowed outside in the sun for four years.

He didn't appear odd or depraved, and I was surprised at how articulate and reflective he was. His biggest mistake in life, he said, was that he had been lazy and lacked direction. In those earlier years, he would rather play volleyball on the beach with his buddies than stick it out in school. He told me he drew strength from his family and the knowledge that he was innocent.

"I don't belong here," he said. The words resonated with me. They were the same ones my mother had spoken more than thirty years before, when we sat on the grass at Camarillo State Hospital. I hadn't believed my mother then, but now I wondered: Could Buckey be telling the truth?

A few weeks later I interviewed his mother, Peggy Buckey, the other principal defendant, in the office of her lawyer. A heavy-set older woman, she told of being forced to submit to periodic strip searches during her two years in jail, and sometimes other inmates tried to set her hair on fire. As we talked, I found her to be one of the kindest, warmest people I had ever met. The scary, depraved images of these people portrayed in the press didn't square with who they seemed to be in person, and from then on I felt an obligation to dig deeper and get their side of the story out to the public.

No publication would give me an assignment, so I investigated the case for six months on my own, taking apart piece by piece the evidence that would be used against the defendants at trial. I concluded there was no credible evidence, only the children's word that these bizarre acts had ever occurred, and their stories were suspiciously similar—digging up dead bodies, faraway trips in airplanes, secret tunnels, cutting the ears off rabbits and the heads off turtles. And the leading questions used by social workers left no way to tell truth from falsehood.

One of the prosecutors eventually talked to me, off the record at first, confiding that the lead prosecutors had rejected all evidence that tended to support the defendants' innocence. Later I got a tip that the chief prosecutor, Lael Rubin, was living with the Metro editor of the *Los Angeles Times* who oversaw the McMartin coverage, a conflict of interest that shocked me. My source had given me their address in Santa Monica, and on trash day, I rifled through black plastic bags on the sidewalk and found bills addressed to both their names. I wrote a story about them in the *Los Angeles Daily Journal,* and later the editor's superiors moved him to another position at the paper.

I became increasingly convinced that Buckey and his mother had been falsely accused. Thinking about the injustice made me burn inside, and at times I thought I'd explode. The McMartins had been a successful, middle-class family, respected by everybody in their community and with a well-known and highly regarded pre-school that had been in the family for three generations. And then, almost overnight, they had been transformed into quintessential underdogs who lost their freedom, their home, their life savings, and the preschool. To help pay their legal bills, the family was forced to turn over the deed to one of their lawyers. He had the school bulldozed and sold the property to a condominium developer.

I felt great empathy for them. They were decent, kind, and loving people, their lives ruined by police, prosecutors, and reporters who were driven by arrogance, ambition, and bad judgment. Never before had I confronted a situation with such gravity and importance, and it opened the window on how mistakes are made in the criminal justice system. I agonized over it, astounded that people in positions of power didn't stop the case from moving forward. The truth didn't seem to matter.

My boyfriend, Gary, threatened to break up with me, saying I had become obsessed, which I suppose I had. At parties I sometimes got into arguments with people over the case. How could they accept wholesale what the media were telling them? Where was their skepticism, their intelligence? How could they actually believe that these defendants had taken the children for airplane rides, through car washes, all the while molesting them, without the parents ever knowing it? Surely at least one of them would have noticed something strange going on long ago.

Along the way I met a kindred spirit, Bob Williams, a veteran reporter at the *Los Angeles Times* who shared my belief that the defendants were innocent and the case was a huge miscarriage of justice. He tried to get the paper's top editors to reconsider its pro-prosecution coverage of the case. In his own work on the case, he had concluded that a few people, driven by their own selfish interests, had unleashed the same hounds of hysteria that ravaged innocent people in the era of McCarthyism in the 1950s and in the witch hunts in Salem in the seventeenth century and in the Middle Ages.

He quoted a statement by defense attorney Joseph Welch that ended the power of Senator Joseph McCarthy: "Have you no sense of decency, sir?" Welch said quietly. "At long last, have you left no sense of decency?"

Williams gave me copies of the preschool's attendance records he had found. To us, they proved that Buckey was nowhere around the preschool when three of the nine child witnesses at his trial testified that he had sexually molested them.

With the attendance records and other evidence I had found, I went to the *New York Times, Vanity Fair,* and *Newsweek* and tried to persuade them to publish a story that presented, for the first time, the "other side of the story." A basic tenant of journalism is to report both sides of a dispute, so I figured they would have me rush a story into print.

"You decide for yourself," I said to Robert Reinhold, West Coast bureau chief of the *Times*. "See if you don't think there's been a huge mistake." Reinhold asked me to write a story on speculation. My lead sentence:

Three of the child witnesses slated to testify in the McMartin Preschool child molestation trial claim Ray Buckey molested them during a time period when the chief defendant was not teaching at the preschool, school attendance records show.

It was an important, explosive story based on authoritative documents. It was big news, and yet the paper's editors in New York turned it down. They said it was too "pro-defense" and needed to be more balanced, which astounded me. There wasn't the same concern about appearing pro-prosecution—the slant most newspapers took. "What if he ends up being convicted?" one of them said. "Then how will we look?" It wasn't possible to be balanced in this story anymore—giving equal time to the defense and prosecution—and still get the truth out. I began to question whether objectivity in journalism—or juries—was ever really possible because human beings are subjective creatures. We are not clean slates; we are the sum of all our experiences and biases.

The *Times'* decision made me even more determined to get the true story out to the public. I remember thinking, *Where is their outrage? How can these editors stand by and do nothing when the system has clearly made a mistake and these people are sitting in jail?*

Bob Williams and I also had meetings with editors at the *Orange County Register* and the *Los Angeles Herald Examiner* (before the paper folded). The editors thought we had uncovered compelling evidence that could tear down the case against the

McMartins, but they were also afraid of appearing biased toward the defense.

Finally, in 1989, I met with an editor, Lew Harris, of *Los Angeles* magazine, who said, "Write the story—on spec—and if you can convince me, I'll publish it." I wrote feverishly for two weeks and in the end, Harris published it with the headline: THE TRUTH ABOUT MCMARTIN. It was the first journalistic account in print to take the position that there was no credible evidence against the defendants, and the story generated national media attention and helped to turn the tide in favor of the defense.

On the day the verdicts came back, hundreds of people pushed toward the courtroom doors hoping to get a seat. We were all part of history in the making that day. This was the dramatic finale to the six-year-ordeal that had come to be called "the crime of the century." In the courtroom I saw Ray Buckey sitting at the counsel table like a stone, a posture he had come to perfect over the years to hide any trace of emotion. If found guilty, he faced decades in prison. His expression changed to a skewered map of joy, disbelief, and sadness when the jury announced that it had found him not guilty on fifty-two of the counts against him, but was deadlocked on thirteen remaining charges. His mother, Peggy Buckey, dabbed at her eyes as she heard her fate: not guilty on all counts.

On the following day, January 19, 1990, the *Los Angeles Times* ran a front-page story with the banner headline MCMARTIN VERDICT: NOT GUILTY, and a lead paragraph with the word JUSTICE.

On the left side of the page, in a Column One report headlined WHERE WAS SKEPTICISM IN MEDIA? *Times* reporter David Shaw began a series of articles on the "Pack journalism and hysteria [that] marked early coverage of the McMartin case. Few journalists stopped to question the believability of the prosecution's charges," he wrote. The series won him a Pulitzer Prize, while Bob Williams, the reporter who first questioned the paper's biased reporting, had been suspended without pay for two days and later resigned and moved to the desert to write books.

Ray Buckey was retried two months after the first verdict, and a new jury deadlocked again. Ira Reiner, the district attorney, declined to order another trial, and the remaining charges against Buckey were dropped. He was finally free.

Some people said, "See, the system worked," but I always bristled when I heard that. It wasn't true. If the system had worked as it should have, the McMartin defendants would never have been arrested or charged, let alone gone on trial. From my experiences on the case, I found my voice, once so faint and uncertain, now clear and definite. I saw up close how easily reporters, police, and prosecutors made mistakes, yet there was no accountability. That was the real crime in this case—innocent peoples' lives were ruined, and there was never any accountability. The family filed civil suits against the main players but never received a dime, or an apology.

As a journalist, I learned the value of persistence, of independent thinking, of using one's instinct, of not following the pack down the track to a woeful ending.

And from the dignity the McMartins demonstrated in the face of enormous adversity, I saw the power and strength that can arise when members of a family love one another and stick together.

People still ask me what became of the McMartins. Virginia

McMartin died a year or so after the case ended, and her daughter
Peggy Buckey died in 2000. At her memorial service, her son-in-law
spoke eloquently about how the family had moved on from the or-
deal and found peace. Old memories had faded from their minds as
they picked up and went on with their lives. I saw Ray Buckey
there. He looked fit, tanned, and happy, and he had become philo-
sophical: "In another five years or so," he said, "most people won't
even know the name Buckey."

Last year the *Los Angeles Times* ran a first-person story by
"Kyle," one of the child witnesses who accused the Buckeys. In his
thirties now, his conscience had weighed heavily on him, and he felt
the need to apologize. In the story he said he had "made it all up"
and went on to explain the reasons most people had already come to
accept—pressure from his parents and police, leading questions
from social workers who lured him into making accusations against
McMartin teachers.

"I'm sorry," he said. His apology came too late to make up for
what had ravaged the lives of the McMartins and many other innocent families.

But it added a note of closure.

On the plane to Atlanta in 1992, I was deeply concerned about Scout, as I was every time I had to leave town on an assignment. Anyone who noticed me in the airport, or saw me peering into a book in my seat on the plane, would have thought I was just another cramped passenger trying to make the best of the conditions. But inside I was a wreck, worried that something would go wrong and I would lose my precious dog.

It was a bad case of separation anxiety, an eruption of feelings from the past when I did lose loved ones. I was paying a friend to look after her, but you just never know. Workmen and meter readers sometimes forgot to close gates, according to stories I'd been told, and the owner's dogs ran away and were never found. And there were other stories of dogs that ran into the street and were killed by cars, or slipped out of their leashes in a park and couldn't find their way home. After a couple of days, I calmed down and focused on my assignment.

In the spring of 1992, I was in Atlanta to do a story for *Vanity Fair* about the three high-profile lawyers—Alan Dershowitz, William Kunstler, and Georgia's Bobby Lee Cook—who were trying to get a new trial for Wayne Williams, the so-called Atlanta child murderer.

After the McMartin story, I felt driven to investigate other criminal cases that were also surrounded by controversy. McMartin had taught me to look for the deeper story behind the official version, and by going against the grain, I might uncover a more accurate and compelling story. As I studied the evidence that supported twenty-nine charges of murder against Williams, I found similarities between the two cases in terms of how the investigations and trials had been conducted. I thought Williams might not be guilty of all of the charges; surely the criminal justice system couldn't have made that big of a mistake again. But at the same time, I couldn't be certain that he was completely innocent.

The hounds of hysteria were unleashed in Atlanta in 1980 when it appeared that a phantom serial killer had begun a senseless slaughter of the city's children. The case was the biggest news story to come out of the South since the assassination of Martin Luther King, Jr., in Memphis in 1968. At first, police tended to ignore the killings—in part because the victims were black and poor. But as the toll of gruesome murders rose to the official total of twenty-nine, public fear and outrage, magnified by intense media coverage, generated a manhunt unparalleled in modern times.

As the months passed without a solution to a single case, pressure to find the killer became so intense that, as a mayoral aide put it, "The city was about to explode." No one was above suspicion. Neighbor suspected neighbor, ex-spouses viewed each other warily. In addition to the human loss, Atlanta's image as a national convention center began to sink. The city's leaders wanted results—and they wanted them fast. Atlanta could no longer wait for justice. It needed a resolution. A scapegoat.

It was in this crazed, charged atmosphere that Wayne Williams, a cocky, ambitious, twenty-eight-year-old DJ and record promoter, emerged as a suspect. Late one foggy night in 1981, he was on his way home, driving over the James Jackson Parkway Bridge that stretched over the Chattahoochee River, when he was stopped by an FBI agent and three Atlanta police who had been staked out under the bridge. Two of the victims had been found dead in the river, and officials believed the killer would return to drop another body there.

Williams always professed his innocence, but even before he was arrested, his chance at a fair trial was lost when the press staked out his house and published his name and home address, creating a widespread belief that he was the killer.

From then on investigators focused single-mindedly on Williams, although there were other, more likely suspects. In the story I ultimately published in *GQ,* I wrote about the secret, so-called 8100 police file (leaked to me by a police insider) that identified a family of Ku Klux Klan members in the area as probable suspects in at least two of the murders. Investigators wiretapped the members' phones and heard such incriminating statements as "Let's go out and kill us another black kid." Yet police suppressed the information, fearing it might cause a race riot, my source told me.

In 1982, Williams was found guilty of killing two adults—the young men found in the river—but he was never convicted of killing any of the twenty-seven child victims, although the label of Atlanta's child murderer stuck to him. Investigators built the case on scientifically unreliable fiber "evidence"—single strands from carpeting and a bedspread found in Williams' home and car that state and FBI experts testified "matched" or were "similar to" fibers found on some of the victims.

DNA testing had not yet been introduced in trials, and forensic science in general was in its infancy. Now, more than twenty years later, were the fibers to be analyzed again with more precise, present-day testing methods, I doubt there could be the same testimony, as the primitive methods once used have now been largely discredited in the scientific community.

In addition, prosecutors could supply no eyewitnesses, no fingerprints, no murder weapons, and no credible person who had ever seen Williams near any of the victims. They also could find no motive other than the theory that Williams was a sociopath, a theory that was never established by any evidence.

After the trial, law enforcement officials stood on the steps of the Fulton County Courthouse in front of media cameras and announced that the case was officially closed. They were attributing the other twenty-seven murders to Williams, even though he hadn't been indicted or tried for any of them. Their decision astounded me. Prosecutors could never get away with it today, and from my viewpoint, the two murders blamed on Williams remain unsolved, along with the horrible deaths of those twenty-seven children.

I interviewed dozens of people in Atlanta connected to the case and reviewed thousands of case file pages, and came to believe that there was no one serial killer. The twenty-nine murders were not connected, as authorities claimed, but rather they resulted from four common causes of homicides: drug deals gone bad, sex for hire, racial hatred, and domestic violence.

Williams, now approaching the age of fifty, is still in prison, and his new lawyer is trying to get him a new trial based on the evidence in the 8100 file that was never turned over to Williams's original defense team.

When I think of his case, I'm reminded of the frightening power of the authorities and the media once they have stirred up public hysteria. Then they can trample over the innocent in the pursuit of wrongdoers, real or imagined, and manipulate evidence to "prove" their case. When that happens, the criminal justice system opens the road to injustice.

If there was a lesson here, it was this: If false, unfounded accusations could devastate the lives of the Buckeys, the McMartins, and Wayne Williams, it could happen to anyone.

In 2005, the police chief of De Kalb County, where several of the child murders occurred, reopened five of the cases, saying he has long believed Williams is innocent. Retesting the fibers will hopefully be part of the new probe, and time will tell if the criminal justice system in Georgia is ready to admit its mistake and free Williams. There's an important story to be told about how so many people could have been so wrong, and the influences—racial, political, and social—that drove the press and law enforcement to this trial by ambush.

A call from Art Cooper, *GQ*'s editor in chief, came in October 1994, after my story on the secret 8100 file ran. I was on deadline writing another story for *GQ*, about the 1993 Michael Jackson molestation scandal. "We'll send you anywhere you want to go," he said. "Just keep doing what you're doing." I accepted his offer to be a senior writer on the magazine's staff, and that began the glory days in my journalism career. I traveled pretty much wherever I wanted to pursue interesting stories. On Saipan and the beautiful island of Palau, in the Caroline Islands, I looked into the battle over DHL co-founder Larry Hillblom's fortune after he died in a plane crash. Traveling to England and Brussels, I investigated surveillance abuses by the National Security Agency's global spying system, called ECHELON. In Burma, after a DEA agent discovered his CIA cronies had hidden a bug in his living room so they could stay in the loop about who his informants were, he sued the agency for illegal eavesdropping. I almost lost the story when the DEA agent, fearing reprisals, refused to talk to me, but after hounding him for several months, he finally came around.

I went to Bangkok to interview a TV producer from the United States who'd been caught at the Bangkok airport with seven pounds of heroine tucked in the lining of his suitcase. He had been sentenced to death, but after begging for his life and proclaiming his innocence—he insisted that he'd been coerced into carrying the drugs—his sentence was reduced, and he was serving eight years in Bangkok's most squalid prison, a rat- and worm-infested place where inmates ate rice and fish heads. I had to bribe two guards to get in, but unable to communicate about how much money they wanted, I opened my wallet and they each took a fifty-dollar bill.

I went to New York and Washington, D.C., many times for one investigative story or another, including one about corruption in the FBI crime lab and another about the Justice Department's habit of launching investigations of black politicians more often than those who were white. In 1996, I made the first of many trips to Oklahoma City to investigate the mysterious death of Kenneth Trentadue, who'd been found hanging in his cell in a federal prison there. Guards claimed he had committed suicide, but when his family saw his bruised and battered body, they embarked on a long fight—which is still going on more than a decade later—with the Justice Department and the FBI to prove Trentadue was murdered by guards.

I wrote two stories for *GQ* about the case, in one naming the FBI agent who had left bloody clothing from Trentadue's cell—crucial DNA evidence that may have established the identity of his attackers—in the trunk of his government car and then forgot about it for two weeks. In the hot Oklahoma sun, the evidentiary value of the items was destroyed. After the story came out, the agent sued me and Condé Nast for defamation, claiming I had accused him of a cover-up in Trentadue's death, and the case went to trial in 2004.

For the first time I found myself in front of a courtroom being grilled on the witness stand, and I didn't much like it. In the end, the jurors found in my favor. "It's definitely a victory for the First Amendment," my lawyer, Bob Nelon, told reporters in the hallway, "and the ability for our media to comment on and, if necessary, criticize our government."

By the time I began reporting on the Michael Jackson case for *GQ* in January 1994, it appeared to be over. Jackson, in avoiding a civil trial, had paid millions of dollars to a thirteen-year-old boy (and his parents) who had accused the superstar of sexually molesting him. My experience in the McMartin case aroused my suspicions that there might be more to the story than what had been reported. But I figured that all the available information had been picked over by reporters, and there was probably nothing left to discover.

Since most of the media were chasing Jackson and his camp, I decided to look in the other direction—at the people who had made the allegations against Jackson, starting with the boy's father and his lawyer, Barry Rothman. After poring over stacks of court documents and business records and interviewing scores of people, including one "deep throat" source who met me in out-of-the-way restaurants and sent me revealing documents in envelopes with no return address, I came up with a radically different story than the one being promoted by the press. My investigation seemed to suggest that Jackson may have molested no one and had himself been the victim of a well-conceived plan to extract money from him.

One important piece of evidence came to me casually, when I was having lunch with the lawyer for the boy's mother at an Italian restaurant in the San Fernando Valley. As we were discussing the case, he said, "That was the day they gave Jordi [the young accuser] the drug." Had I heard correctly? What drug? It was a reporter's dream moment come true. Here was important information that had not yet been reported. With more digging, I found a second source who said the drug—sodium amytal, a powerful psychiatric drug—had been administered intravenously to the boy by a friend of his father's, a dental anesthesiologist who I discovered was under investigation by the DEA for administering drugs illegally. Only after the boy had been given the drug, known to make people under its influence receptive to suggestion, did he tell a psychiatrist that Jackson had molested him, according to my sources.

The story ran on *GQ*'s cover with the headline WAS MICHAEL JACKSON FRAMED? THE UNTOLD STORY. When the magazine hit the stands in October 1994, my story became *the* story, as it was the first to present a defense of Jackson. I had dozens of TV and radio interviews. My stock at the magazine was never higher. My editors let me buy a fifteen-hundred-dollar Richard Tyler suit (on sale from three thousand dollars), and they hired a limo to take me to all my interviews.

My hunches had paid off. The story became a finalist for the National Magazine Award, and, for the first time, I came to know what fame felt like.

Regardless of what opinion people have about Jackson, objectivity and restraint were again casualties of the crazed, sensationalism that hounded him in 2005, when he was tried—and found not guilty—on child molestation charges. His case made TV careers for several personalities who seemed to trade fairness for ambition.

In looking back over the last decade to what has brought the media itself to scandal, where its inaccuracies and excesses are now often the subject of news, where many people no longer trust or have faith in it, it seems some of its members have made that same Faustian bargain, trading fairness and ethics for ego and ambition. High-profile mistakes like McMartin, like Wayne Williams, like accused Chinese spy Wen Ho Lee, and like accused Atlanta Olympic bomber Richard Jewell might never have gotten as far as they did, and the suspects would not have been so vilified and their lives ruined, had reporters used common sense and employed qualities they often shun—skepticism and restraint.

Empathy and instinct certainly shouldn't override reliable facts, but after seeing the harm done by their absence, I think now that no determination about an individual or a case or a defendant should be made on cold facts alone. Wisdom, it seems to me, derives from drawing on everything you've learned in life, all your experiences, and what's in your heart.

32

As it turned out, I didn't have to fly around the country and visit people in prison to find cases of injustice; there were some right in my own neighborhood, just in a different form.

It's important here to understand a little bit about my neighborhood so my actions will make sense. I live in one of the oldest parts of Los Angeles, on the affordable but funky east side of town. It's so far east, even east of Dodger Stadium, that for a long time many of my friends—most of them westsiders—had never heard of the area, let alone been here.

When they finally do come, some of them sit on my couch and look out the big bay window, making sure their car isn't stolen. Call it many things—eclectic, artsy, up and coming, multiethnic—my community is all that, but there's no getting around the reality that it's also the hood. At times the air crackles with gunfire, and police helicopters circle over our yards, looking for some burglar or gang-banger. Competing gangs mark their territory with black graffiti. Old mattresses, couches, and an occasional toilet sit on sidewalks until someone gets tired of looking at them and calls the city bulk trash department. For me, the hardest thing is watching stray dogs and cats wandering the streets, dodging cars as they look for scraps of food.

One day, when I drove to the 7-Eleven store near my house, I saw a small black cat peering into the store window, presumably looking for food. In the past, I never would have considered taking in a cat—I wasn't that fond of them—but I couldn't leave her there and still live with my conscience. So I took her home, named her Sammie, and fell in love with her. My world was expanding in ways I hadn't expected. How could I have missed the wonder of cats? I thought.

Another time, a few blocks from my house, I saw a small black dog confined in the cruelest way I'd ever seen. The owner's yard was completely fenced in, and yet they had constructed a small cage in one corner, locked the dog inside it, and constricted him even further with a four-foot chain attached to his collar so all the poor animal could do was stand up and sit down. I couldn't understand how they could let their dog live in such harsh, restrictive conditions. Didn't they care? I tried talking to the owners, nicely, but when they didn't correct the situation, I called the Humane Society and an animal investigator came, seized the dog, and placed him in a new home.

My neighborhood is a mix of people from El Salvador, Mexico, Vietnam, and the Philippines—along with Caucasians—and most of the time, we all "get along," the idealized scenario Rodney King begged us to practice, after he was beaten eighty-one times over his head and body by four city police officers.

Sometimes, though, our neighborhood values clash, as when my neighbor around the corner, a woman from El Salvador, had a rooster in her backyard that kept waking me up at five o'clock every morning. The noise didn't bother her; she had lived on a farm in

El Salvador and was used to it. But I wasn't. I reported her to the Department of Animal Regulation (it forbids keeping farm animals in urban areas), and my neighbor responded to the complaint by cutting off the bird's head—as she used to do in her country when it was time for a holiday feast. I felt guilty about my part in the rooster's demise, but rationalized it as being necessary to restore peace and quiet to the neighborhood.

I don't go looking for trouble around here. Yet one evening in 1995, there it was, right across the street, a dog shrieking. I looked out my kitchen window. A neighbor, a big man with huge biceps, was beating his dog, a black cocker spaniel named Ruby. She cowered in the corner of the small front yard, shaking and whimpering as he smacked her hard across the face and body.

My body filled with adrenaline even as my mind shied away from getting involved. Having stolen Charlie, I knew how stressful such ventures could be, yet I couldn't stop myself. Something had to be done. But what? I didn't want to antagonize the neighbor who lived so close to me. So I must think of some indirect intervention.

When he was outside washing his car or sweeping the sidewalk, I made a point of walking Scout (she made a perfect decoy) in front of his house so I could strike up friendly conversation. The man told me that Ruby was "a bad girl" because she often got out in the narrow space under the gate.

"Oh, my dog used to do that, too," I lied. "I finally just nailed boards in all her getaway spots."

"Yah, that's what I'll do," my neighbor said, thanking me for the tip. It would have been so simple. All he had to do was nail a single five-foot-long board under the gate and the problem would have been solved. But weeks passed, and he never got around to it.

Ruby kept getting out like dogs do, and my neighbor continued beating her, sometimes with his six-year-old daughter watching him. In my mind, I pleaded with her to speak out—as I wished I had done with my father all those years ago. But she just stood there and watched. Meanwhile, I couldn't concentrate on my magazine assignments. Something had to be done. So I started devising a plan to steal Ruby, but images of the little girl across the street kept getting in the way. I remembered how devastated I was when I lost Queenie, so I wanted to consider her feelings.

Torn by my dilemma, I called my friend Carmen for advice. Whatever she said I would abide by, I told myself. Her moral standards were higher than those of anyone I knew. For fifteen years she had lived as a nun in the Self-Realization Fellowship, and she was the most spiritually evolved person I had ever met.

"Normally I'd say it's not right to take something that doesn't belong to you," she told me. "But in this situation, I'd say that whatever promotes love is the best course of action to take."

Over the next few days I carried out my plan. I enlisted the help of Sharon, a college student I knew who loved dogs. I paid her twenty-five dollars to stay close to her phone in the evenings over the next few days. Then I watched out my kitchen window, and when I saw my neighbor's family get in their car and drive away, I called her.

"OK, let's do it," I said. I walked casually in front of my neighbor's house, then bent down as if I were looking for something on the sidewalk—maybe my contact lens. After several cars passed by, I pulled bits of steak out of my pocket and waved them under the gate. Sure enough, Ruby wriggled out and I grabbed her. I carried her to the corner where Sharon was waiting in her car and put Ruby in the backseat. And off they went.

The perfect crime. No witnesses. No evidence. Just an empty dirt yard and the space under the gate where my neighbor would think Ruby had slipped out for good. Sharon kept Ruby at her sorority house for a few weeks until the Thanksgiving break, when she and a friend drove Ruby to her parent's house in Washington State. It had a huge backyard with apples trees. And that's where Ruby stayed.

I was surprised by how rewarding the adventure made me feel. Whenever I looked across the street and saw Ruby gone, I felt ecstatic, as if I had suddenly come into a large sum of money. It was a different kind of success, unpaid and risky, but deeply satisfying.

My skills as an investigative reporter had come in handy: a bit of surveillance from the kitchen window, patience, perseverance, and knowing how to get access to an inaccessible source. My editor at *GQ* used to tell people that I was a "fearless" reporter. I wasn't, but I never told him that. I sometimes got nervous when I interviewed political heavyweights like Senator Orrin Hatch and Dick Thornburgh, the former attorney general. At one point I flew to Houston, hoping the retired warden of the federal prison where Kenneth Trentadue had died would talk to me. He wasn't expecting me, nor did he know me, and when I knocked on the front door of his house on a Saturday afternoon, my heart was racing. He ended up letting me in, and we talked for more than an hour.

When it came to dognapping, however, I had no fear.

After Ruby came Sonny, the dog I mentioned earlier, and now I'll tell you the full story of what happened that night. I'm going into detail about it to give you an idea of the pitfalls that await you should you ever consider rescuing abused animals yourself. And truth be told, I'm proud of my venture with Sonny, and look on it as one of my biggest triumphs in life.

This time it was my neighbor Hank, who lived around the corner. He was a hefty man in his midforties with a big beer belly and a dragon tattoo on his right arm. Much of the time he looked rumpled, with days-old stubble, and I couldn't figure out if he had just woken or was coming off some bender.

As a teenager he had been in a gang, but he dropped out when he got married and had his first son. Later he did time for selling drugs out of his house, and another time the police hauled him away after his wife called 911 to report him for beating her. She finally left him a year or so after she had another son.

Hank usually took his rage out on Sonny, a three-year-old yellow Lab mix, strong and sturdy, with rich brown eyes and white hair on his chest, and paws that looked as if he were wearing socks. I had never seen a dog so exuberant, so determined to connect to life, and I was continually awed by his spirit and indomitable will to be free. As a puppy, he had been a stray roaming the streets of my neighborhood until one morning he walked up Hank's street and had the misfortune of being spotted by him. I happened to be out walking that morning with Scout when I saw Hank pull Sonny into his house by the hair on his neck.

I shuddered thinking what lay in store for the poor dog. Hank couldn't care less about dogs, but he took the puppy in as a belated birthday present for his sons. Soon, however, they got tired of playing with Sonny, and from then on the dog lived as a prisoner locked behind a wire gate in a narrow strip of dirt filled with old tools and bags of used bottles and cans. Never once did I see Hank walk Sonny, and on a few occasions when he went away for the weekend, he never bothered to leave food and water.

On my walks around the neighborhood, I saw a microcosm of our alienated culture—yard after yard of mostly solitary dogs, napping, isolated from each other, yearning for connection. I thought how wonderful it would be if the dogs could meet up in a central location and play with each other all day, then return to their owners at night.

When I walked by Hank's house, I would see Sonny sitting in the same place behind the gate, his tail wagging with expectation, as if any moment the gate would open and he would be set free to have a normal life, playing with Scout and the other dogs in the neighborhood. I tried to remain detached, turning away when I passed by, but it was no use. I usually stopped, made small talk with Hank, and gave him biscuits and rawhide treats to give to Sonny.

As Sonny grew older, the isolation became intolerable, and he found clever ways to break free. Once I found blood caked around his neck and figured he had used his head as a kind of drilling tool to enlarge a small hole in the wire gate. I wiped the blood off with a mild antiseptic and rewarded his bravery with several tasty biscuits, a ritual I honored each time he made a stop at my house, which was any chance he got. I cheered when I saw Sonny roaming free, knowing that for a few minutes, anyway, he was enjoying some measure of happiness. Yet I also cringed, knowing what fate awaited him when Hank came home.

He would always drag Sonny back by the collar, beat him and kick him hard in the ribs, then lock him behind the gate again. It was criminal how Hank treated Sonny. I witnessed some of the beatings, as did my neighbors, but we were afraid to confront Hank directly. "Waddya goin' ta do?" one neighbor said, shrugging his shoulders.

The injustice of the situation resurrected memories from my past and ate away at me as almost nothing else could.

This happened in 1998, when I was living with Gary, another good-looking charmer who hated confrontations and refused to get involved with my dog adventures. He's the one who told me to "let the authorities handle it. It's not your business." In my experience, bureaucracies were rarely helpful, but I called the Department of Animal Regulation anyway. An officer told me an inspector would have to catch Hank in the act of beating Sonny, and failing that, I would have to testify against Hank in open court—a scenario that was completely out of the question, since my identity would be revealed and Hank would undoubtedly retaliate. I imagined my house firebombed, my car battered, and Scout and Sammie poisoned.

Nevertheless, earlier that fall, when Hank began locking Sonny in the small shed underneath his house, I started devising a plan. I asked my friend Bonnie for help this time. She lived a mile from me, and we had met at the college while walking our dogs. She was as intolerant as I was about animals being abused. "Of course, I'll help," she said. "Just tell me what I need to do."

Accomplices were hard to come by in these clandestine ventures, so I was grateful for her help—even though she might not be able to carry out her part in the mission. She was a high-strung, jittery woman who became disoriented in times of stress; not the best of traits in this line of work, but I knew of no other volunteers.

For a week I conducted surveillance from my kitchen window to determine patterns in Hank's schedule. My house was on a hill and gave me a direct sight to the front of his house. His sons came home on the weekends, and daytime was clearly not a possibility. His blue truck stayed parked on the street most of the day, indicating he was once again out of work. I noticed, though, that he left his house for twenty, sometimes thirty minutes late at night. I surmised he went out to sell drugs, but whatever the reason, I knew his absence then was my only window of opportunity.

I waited and I watched. Then one Tuesday night around ten o'clock I saw him drive away. *Finally,* I thought. I was already dressed in my black sweatpants and turtleneck, and I quickly put some dog biscuits and a leash in a small black knapsack and headed for the front door. "He'll know it's you," my boyfriend said. "You could go to jail." Since I had befriended Sonny, and Hank had often found him in front of my house, waiting for me to come out, I knew I would be the prime suspect. But the time for caution was over. And besides, I was confident of my thieving skills and knew that Hank, not I, was the real criminal in this situation.

I walked to the corner and waved to Bonnie. She would wait five minutes and then start my car's engine. As I proceeded around the corner to Hank's house, I felt strongly motivated, unafraid, and eager to complete my mission. I climbed over his fence and tiptoed across his yard to the wire gate that Sonny always sat behind, then raised the latch and started down the steps toward the shed. When I heard a car pull up and stop, my heart started beating wildly. It must be Hank. I dropped to the ground as my mind raced. What would I say if he caught me? So far I could only be charged with trespassing, a misdemeanor, but I could probably talk my way out of it, if I had a reasonable explanation. My cat! I would say that Sammie had wandered across the street toward his house and I had gone looking for her. A feeble excuse, but it would have to do.

I crouched down in the dirt and waited. Sonny's moist, black nose pushed out from under the shed door. "Shh," I said softly. He must have known it was me bumping around in the dark because he never once barked. Suddenly the car accelerated up the street and was gone.

I worked quickly. First, I jimmied the padlock on the shed door. Sonny bounded out of the small, windowless space and licked my cheek. I stroked his head and reached in my pack and gave him a biscuit. He gobbled it up in a few seconds, and I gave him another one while I attached the leash around his neck. We were about to go up the stairs when his back foot stepped on a rake, toppling it against the neighbor's fence. I froze and pressed Sonny close as their bedroom light turned on. We waited a few minutes until the room went dark again, then started back up the stairs. As we crossed through the front yard, and I unlatched the gate from the inside, I purposely left both gates ajar to make it look as if Sonny had once again managed to get out.

We walked quickly down the street. As we turned the corner, I didn't see Bonnie right away and panicked. Had she gotten cold feet and deserted me at a critical moment? Just then headlights flashed from up the street. She had moved my car and was now parked on the opposite side, headed north instead of south. I pulled Sonny across the street as the only eyewitness, a brown chow, barked ferociously. Bonnie opened the passenger door and Sonny jumped in the backseat.

We sped off into the night, our hearts racing, our eyes peeled for Hank's truck. When we were safely out of range, I lowered the back window, and Sonny put his head out into the cool night air, savoring his first moments of freedom. Few things compared to the perfect joy of that moment, and I felt profound satisfaction that Sonny was now free to begin a happy life.

When Hank came home later that night and found Sonny missing from the shed, he did end up suspecting me, but he could never prove I was the culprit. Leaving the two gates ajar was like a stroke of genius, since it created reasonable doubt in his mind. Still, two days later he cornered me on the street in front of my house and bore in so close that the tips of our shoes touched. He tried intimidating me into confessing, huffing and slinging accusations, but I held firm, denying that I knew anything about Sonny's disappearance.

"I'm sure he'll come back," I said in a friendly tone, knowing full well that Sonny had already begun a new life in paradise. Bonnie agreed to let him stay with her two dogs in her large, grassy yard until I found a permanent home for Sonny. But, as I had hoped, she became attached to Sonny and ended up keeping him.

I suppose Hank had a right to be upset. Two other dogs of his had also disappeared mysteriously, one before Sonny and one after, and the truth is, I stole them, too, and found them loving homes. One was a sweet, chubby brown puppy, part pit bull, part Lab. I saw Hank kick the puppy a few times to get him up the stairs, and I refused to let it happen again. That time, after I saw Hank drive away, I put on a scarf and carried a small duffel bag down his side stairs. The puppy was happy to have the company, and I scooped him up in my arms and put him in the bag.

The other one, Sue, a six-year-old boxer mix, wasn't as easy. I had to dig out under the fence in back of Hank's house and carefully pull Sue out.

After all his dogs disappeared, Hank went to the pound and got two more mutts—a Dalmatian and a German shepherd. Why did he keep getting dogs, I wondered, when he clearly didn't want to take care of them—or even like them? Maybe he used them as an alarm system. Or maybe it was about power. His life was a failure, and dogs were the one thing he had control over. He could treat them anyway he pleased. Sadly, until the animal welfare laws changed and stopped classifying animals as peoples' property, as slaves had been viewed, Hank and others like him could continue their crimes against the innocent.

But he seemed to treat these dogs better. None of my neighbors ever saw him hit them, and for a while I thought he had finally gotten the message: If he abused and neglected his dogs, he was going to lose them.

33

What you discover fairly quickly when you do this kind of thing with any regularity is that there are other people who do it, too. After I swiped Sue from Hank, I couldn't find him (Sue was a him) a home right away, and I pleaded for help from anyone I could think of who was even remotely connected to animals. I couldn't keep Sue for the obvious reason—my proximity to the scene of the crime (Hank's house)—so after many desperate phone calls, I was introduced to the underground world of animal rescue, a vast, unorganized network of men and women who are passionately concerned about animals being abused and neglected.

I started my search with my friend Bonnie. She had already taken in Sonny and transformed her yard into a small zoo with four dogs and four cats, so I knew I probably had already shot my wad, but I tried anyway. "I just can't take any more, Mary," she said. "I'm sorry." I would hear that a lot.

I went to see the technician at my vet's office, a beautiful young woman with long blond hair who could easily get any man she wanted, yet she preferred to spend her free time finding good homes for dogs and cats. "Take a photo of the dog; that's the first step," she said, "and I'll see what I can do."

As I would discover, there are different types of animal rescuers, and the blond tech fit into two categories: She used her many contacts to try to place animals, and sometimes she also scanned the city's pounds and shelters and rescued dogs, cats, birds, rabbits, whatever from their cages at the midnight hour, just before they were about to be euthanized. People like her are called the "angels" of pet rescue.

Other rescuers turn their houses and yards into specialty kennels, rescuing only certain breeds of dogs from the streets and impending death. The more they take in, the greater the cost. Some end up going into debt, some are evicted, and city officials, on a tip from a disgruntled neighbor, raid their homes and seize their animals. As I scanned the *Pet Press,* the main animal newspaper, looking for leads, I found a page full of listings of animal rescue groups: chow, beagle, and my favorite, in honor of Scout—schnauzer rescues. I called a couple of rescues that specialized in boxers. "Is he a full-breed boxer?" asked one woman who answered the phone.

"Not exactly," I said, sighing as I realized that Sue's chances were nil. He had the short, pert ears of a boxer, and his head and face had the white markings of the breed, but his body and tail were a hodgepodge of God only knows what.

"I'm sorry," the woman said, "but we are so full that we can only take dogs that are full-breed boxers or close to that."

Then there are the rescuers like me, people who steal animals they discover living in all sorts of terrible conditions. We use the term *rescue* when we talk about our adventures, but we all know it's a euphemism for stealing.

Right under my nose was this parallel universe of modern-day abolitionists and vigilantes who, in their passion to rescue animals from hardship and abuse, took justice into their own hands. These were my kind of people. They didn't look to the "authorities" for help; they took action, becoming judges and juries of one who identified the guilty and freed the innocent.

Frankly, I wish more people would try it, but I know this kind of work isn't for everyone. It requires patience, stealth, cunning, and an abiding intolerance for people like Hank who misuse their power over animals. The tenet that there are no bad dogs, only bad owners, could be our logo if we ever sent out flyers to recruit fellow animal lovers.

Rescue stories help inspire us, but they are hard to hear: dogs tethered to six-foot ropes and chains, their necks permanently scarred, until some brave, caring person climbs over a fence with a big pair of pliers, sets them free, and finds them a good home. Then there are the malnourished dogs with exposed rib bones, others with cigarette burns, beer bottles broken over their heads, or their ears chewed away by mites or other insects.

You have to wonder, as we often do, why in the world do these people have animals in the first place. It's a question of endless frustration because there really is no acceptable answer. Some people see dogs as machines, not living creatures, and they're indifferent to the needs of animals for exercise, nurturing, and decent food. "These people just don't care" is a fairly standard explanation.

I quickly learned not to depend on just one or two people for help in finding Sue a home. As we did at *People* magazine, I "threw out the net." But got no response. Finding homes for stray and rescued animals is about the hardest thing you can do. People are reluctant to take on more responsibility unless they have to. As with magazine freelancing, you have to have many irons in the fire to be successful.

"Make up a flyer with the dog's photo and personal details," a woman who keeps twenty-six cats at her house told me. "Then post it on Internet pet sites." I first met the woman at the college where I walked Charlie and Scout. She had her dog then, an Irish setter named Pups. After he died, she focused her love of animals on cats. Stray cats were everywhere. She rescued them from parking lots, underneath cars, in alleys, in the brush alongside freeway on-ramps. She found kittens, some only days old, abandoned in Dumpsters. To her they were "angels," and she took care of them better than some people do for their own kids.

In making up the flyer, I got a tip from an old pro, a man who had worked at a city animal shelter: "No one wants an old dog. Shave a few year's off his age." So I penned in Sue's age as four instead of six. When I took my flyer to the local pet store, I discovered that Sue would have stiff competition. On the shelf over the cash register hung a gallery of photos of forlorn-looking dogs and cats in need of homes. "You can put your flyer up there," the owner said. "But I can't guarantee you'll get any calls."

Once in a great while you get a yes, which Sue finally got. A woman in Santa Monica, someone I didn't know, had found my flyer on the Internet, fell in love with Sue, picked him up, and took him home.

At this point I should say that all evidence to the contrary, I and many of the other rescuers I've met are not, well, rabid in how we fulfill our mission, at least not in ways you might expect. Admittedly this kind of fringe work attracts odd characters from time to time, like the man I met who hates most people and will only come out of his house to go to the market, afraid his neighbors will climb over his fence and steal his five dogs. From my days in therapy, I know he is "projecting" his own questionable practices on other people.

For the most part, however, I've met interesting, solid people: a vet who will go unnamed, a marketing and branding executive, an NBC publicist, and a former lawyer who now runs Wagville, a dog-boarding and day-care facility that has no cages. Dogs roam free under careful supervision, and there's a Web cam so people can go online and see their dogs when they travel.

I do confess that over the years I've visited animal shelters from time to time, which is how I found Scout. But now I find those places too emotionally wrenching, and I only go when I have to check up on a rescued animal I'm trying to place. And now, when I'm waiting for a massage at a daytime spa near my house, I've been known to pick up *National Geographic* and read its cover story, "Wolf to Woof: The Evolution of Dogs," instead of the latest *Vanity Fair*.

34

The long, winding road we took to get to Camarillo State Hospital was just as I had remembered it more than forty years ago. My friend Jonathan and I drove past the same open fields, planted now with lemon trees. All the cows and chickens were gone, but halfway up the road we saw a yellow diamond-shaped sign: DEER CROSSING. How appropriate, I thought. Mom would have liked that.

I had wanted to visit Camarillo before now but had never felt ready. Now I thought I had to come—to do research for this book, if for nothing else. I wanted to see where Mom had lived and if the place had the same powerful, haunting effect on me that it had when I was six years old.

It was safer to come now, too. There were no more patients, and the mental hospital had closed in 1997. It was being turned into a school: California State University, Channel Islands. The closing had been gradual, starting in 1976, when the Reagan era of social program cutbacks gutted the state's mental health budget and forced mental patients into halfway houses or to their new homes on the streets.

The grounds were just as I remembered them—sweeping

lawns, the beautiful mountains in the background, the magnolia tree where we had sat with Mom, only it was much bigger now. I studied the maze of whitewashed buildings and pink tile roofs, now faded and worn. All the white colors prompted Jonathan to comment, "You know, white is the color of insanity." I hadn't known that, I told him.

Half of the patient wards had been remodeled and converted into classrooms; the others were dark and empty, their heavy metal doors locked. We peered through a door's small square glass window, covered in mesh wiring, into a bare, gray wasteland of sorrow. We strolled around the maze of abandoned wards, now like above-ground catacombs, their dank hollowness arousing what I imagined were the horrors my mother may have endured in those rooms. Farther on, we peeked through a set of windows that had metal bars on both sides. It had probably been the patients' day room. All the furniture was gone; balls of dust, rain-stained boxes, a TV's antenna poking up like a rabbit's ear were now its only occupants.

I spotted a woman who looked as if she knew her way around. She had worked in the administration office at Camarillo for more than fifteen years. I told her that my mother had spent time here and asked, "Are there any patient wards that still exist in the way they were in the old days?"

"Come with me," she said. "I think you might be in luck." We walked back through the maze the other way, into a ward way in the back by the foothills. She unlocked the door, and there before me was the dormitory, or one like it, that had been my mother's home for nine years. The walls were bare concrete, the floor speckled with linoleum. Seven beds were lined up on both sides, making the place look like a military barracks. Mom would have had no privacy. At Ramona Convent, I at least had a curtain to pull around me. Sadness washed over me as I imagined my mother, a grown woman, living in such barren conditions. In losing each other, we had both lived in institutions, only now I saw that she'd had it worse than me.

Months before, I had tried to locate Mom's hospital records. After all these years I still didn't know what her diagnosis was. Camarillo's records had been transferred to another facility, and when I inquired, the woman in the archives said she doubted my mother's records still existed. A few days later she called back. "I've found a three-by-five card with your mother's name on it," she said, "but nothing else." It appeared that all the records from the fifties and before had been destroyed. All that was left of Mom's long existence there had come down to almost nothing, a small white card.

When I received a copy of the card in the mail, I held it for a long time, staring at every typed word as if they held the secret code to understanding my past. It included Mom's name and my father's, her religion—Presbyterian—and the date she was admitted—1956—and her diagnosis: depression.

There it was, finally. The haze lifted. Oh, the tragedy of it, I thought. Had she been diagnosed even fifteen years later, in the seventies, she would have gone for therapy at a psychologist's office, taken an antidepressant, and in a short while would have probably recovered and resumed a normal life with her two young daughters.

How does one make sense of it? A fluke in timing. Her diagnosis made in a decade of primitive psychiatry. No one's fault, really. No one to blame, except maybe the "system"—misguided doctors and technicians who ignored or closed their ears to cries for help from fellow human beings like my mother, warehousing them instead of trying to get them released quickly back to their loved ones.

How do you make sense of life when there's no accountability for injustice? For a long time I wrestled with that universal question. "You have to make peace with the past and go on," Dr. Janos Kalla told me again and again.

As I got older, I didn't have a breakdown like my mother, as my father had once predicted. I had beaten the odds, even through some very tough times. I was different from my mother. I was stronger. A survivor. I wouldn't let a man, even one I deeply loved, derail my life. I could cope with anything and keep moving forward.

When I turned forty-three, I met Bernard. We fell in love, and he moved into my house. He was odd in many ways and eccentric. When I first met him, he wore an ascot and sometimes assumed the character of a British naval officer, speaking in a haughty English accent. He talked more than any other human being I had ever known, even more than my mother, whom I dubbed president of the Yakka Bird Society. Friends of mine didn't know how I could stand Bernard's endless talking. One said she wanted to put a pillow over his head.

But I loved him. He was tender and affectionate. We spoke of traveling to Scotland, of marrying and moving to the countryside in Virginia to run his parents' B and B when they got too old. Some of my best holidays were spent with him. At Christmas we sometimes stayed at a friend's house on the craggy coast above Sonoma, California. We hiked over the rocks, collected unusual shells, and drank champagne as we watched the crimson sunsets. He loved Scout and Sammie and didn't mind them sleeping on the bed with us, an arrangement that other men had trouble with. I took his many nicknames for me as evidence of his love for me, names like acorn, marigold, rosemary, sweedle, tree toes, and kinkajou (a honey bear).

. . .

 ut there were problems, red flags, even from the beginning.
When I first met him at a friend's wedding rehearsal dinner, he
came with another woman, yet he openly flirted with me. "She's a
friend more than a date," he said, and I believed him. Or rather I
wanted to believe that he wouldn't do what my father would have
done in that setting. And I was attracted to him. He was tall and
boyishly handsome, with black hair and classy-looking black-
framed glasses. And he had a playful side. Just my type. He worked
at a small museum in Santa Monica. All very impressive to me, until
I got to know him better.

I came to realize that he was very much like my father—
charming, glib, entertaining, uncommitted, childish. His employers
thought he was strange, unreliable, and he couldn't hold a job for
very long. So I supported him on and off for the seven years we were
together.

"Just don't give away the farm," Dr. Kalla would remind me. In
my case, the "farm" was my house. Bernard thought I should put his
name on the deed because he had paid half the mortgage for a few
months one year.

In August 2001, in a matter of two days, I lost the things that
mattered most to me. On a Monday I learned that after seven wonderful, stimulating years at *GQ,* my job was ending, and on
Wednesday morning Bernard sat down on the bed and said he
was leaving. "But I just lost my job," I said. "You can't leave now. I
need you."

But he did leave. He said he would be living with his friend
Lowell, where he would have to pay his own way, and could
therefore learn to be less dependent on others. But in truth he

moved in with a woman I knew he'd been seeing on the sly. She had money and could support him in the ways he had grown accustomed to. He married her a few months later.

Suddenly all my anchors were gone, and I fell deep into grief, wondering how—or if—I would be able to pull myself out. Many nights I sat outside on my deck, staring into the dark sky, feeling lost and utterly alone. I began smoking cigarettes again after a seventeen-year hiatus. I couldn't sleep or eat and lost twenty pounds. I had to pin the waistband of my skirts and pants with a huge safety pin, and I couldn't stop crying.

"What's the point of going on?" I said to my friend Diana. Day after day, week after week, she patiently listened to my agony, trying to help me make sense of all the loss. "You would have left him eventually," she said. "It's the best thing that could have happened."

One day we were having dinner at her house when it dawned on me. "You know," I said, sniveling, "this is what my mother must have gone through when my father stopped loving her." For the first time I understood the depth of Mom's grief, and my sister's desolation when her lover betrayed her. I understood now how someone could be derailed by loss and infidelity. All of us—my mother, Kate, and now me—had ended up, at different times, at the same juncture in life. Abandoned, alone, questioning the purpose of life, wondering if we had the strength to go on.

Still, I would not give up and collapse in on myself the way my mother had. No man was worth that, I told myself. I would forge ahead.

I returned to freelancing—and therapy—let my hair grow

long, gained back ten pounds, quit smoking, had a passionate affair with a fellow journalist, and threw myself into gardening. I never knew how fulfilling that could be. I brought trunk loads of flowers home and completely relandscaped my front and back yards. The collection of potted cactus Bernard left behind reminded me of him at the end, prickly and austere, and I thought of disposing of them in a Dumpster. But gradually I saw how beautiful and intricate they were, each one different, each one an individual, with its own shape and subtle colors.

And I still had Scout and Sammie. What a comfort they were. When I worked in the garden, they sat outside with me; Scout on the chaise longue, Sammie stretched out on the picnic table where I repotted flowers, playing with the daisies and trailing fuchsia.

As the months passed, Scout began slowing down as her back legs became unsteady. She couldn't run anymore, and her interest in food diminished. Yet I denied the inevitable. She was sixteen, a long life for a dog, but I couldn't imagine my life without her. She was my truest pal, my family, and I denied the end was near. A few weeks passed and she got worse. In the morning her spot on the bed would be wet. Her kidneys were giving out, and I would have to carry her up the front steps when we came back from a walk.

In therapy, I told Dr. Kalla, "I can't bear to lose her. She's everything to me." He was a dog lover himself, and tears came to his eyes when he recounted how he and his wife had been forced to put their two dogs to sleep the year before.

"I wish you would consider going on medication," he said. "I hate to see you suffering like this." For years I had refused his periodic suggestions that I take antidepressants. I didn't need or trust pharmaceuticals. And I wasn't depressed. I wasn't like my mother. I just ran into rough patches now and again.

But facing the loss of Scout made me reconsider. Anything that could help me get through losing her was worth a shot. So I started taking Lexapro, not forever, just for a few months to get me over the hump.

A week later, Scout fell down in the yard and couldn't get back up. She panted heavily, and I knew it was time. I called the vet, and he came to my house. Scout always shook when I took her to the vet, and I wanted her final moments to be as peaceful as possible. I lit a candle in the living room, sat down on the couch, and lifted Scout on my lap. I stroked her sweet face and told her I loved her. Then the vet put in the needle in her front right leg and thirty seconds later her head fell to the side. I wept in the arms of my friend Reyna, who sat beside me. We both wept. My little girl was gone.

I cried on and off for a week or two, and then something extraordinary happened. The medication kicked in and my internal state changed dramatically. I still grieved for Scout, but the pain didn't drag on for months or years—as had all the other major losses in my life. Gone, too, was the fist that used to periodically grip in my chest since my days at Ramona Convent. And I stopped crying. It was as if the foundation of my being, disassembled and left in fragments after my mother had left, was suddenly whole again.

The irony of it all astounded me. And what a rich literary ending for my story. In trying to escape my mother's fate, in trying to distance myself from her experience of shame and sadness, I had blinded my eyes to the reality of my own intermittent struggle with depression. I finally saw it wasn't about strength or weakness; it had to do with brain chemistry. Maybe the depression had started when Mom left me, which would make sense, and I could find no other way to heal the deep wounds of that loss. Or maybe I inherited the depression gene from her.

Either way, it didn't matter anymore.

35

Through my office window at home, I can see my cat, Sammie, resting on top of the lattice over the picnic table, her black fur shining in the warm rays of the morning sun. She stares at the pink camellias and bright yellow hibiscus now in full bloom, but mostly focuses on the hillside behind my house, a well-traveled, grassy thoroughfare for stray cats, keeping an eye out for possible feline intruders into our private domain.

It was only the two of us until a few weeks ago, when I went outside to get the paper and heard a kitten crying. I assumed it was wild, but he walked up and nuzzled his head into my leg. I knew Sammie wouldn't like it, but I hoped in time she would come around and allow the little one to sleep on the bed with us. I named the kitten Ranger because the black around his eyes made it look as if he were wearing a mask, like the Lone Ranger.

One day soon I will buck up, take a deep breath, and walk through the city's shelters to look for another dog. Scout has been gone for a year now, and while I once thought I would never get over losing her and still feel ripples of sadness from time to time, I now look at love and loss in a different way.

People and animals I love continue to come and go from my life, and I am alone in the conventional sense. I have no immediate family, no children, no husband. I received four marriage proposals over the years, but I turned them down for various reasons: I'm not ready, let's give it more time, I don't want to move to San Jose. But underneath I think it's because I'm still skittish about facing the prospect of endings.

After fourteen years, my sister, Kate, and I have still have not seen or talked to each other. Friends tell me I should call her, as I'm sure her friends urge her to call me. Sometimes I think I'll call or write, try to open the closed door between us, but then memories of the past come flooding back and I stop myself. Every part of me rails against going back to the old ways of being. Still, I feel sad knowing that Kate and I have lost each other, neither one knowing how to find our way back. Maybe now, after all these years, the distance between us has made it too far to go back.

And yet I don't feel alone. A year ago, in researching my father's early life, I called my first cousin, Dan Fischer, in Hamilton, Ohio. He is my father's nephew, but we had not spoken in more than forty years. I was reluctant to call him at first, afraid I might get sucked into another unhappy family situation. Over the months we spoke many times, and I was introduced to a whole other side of the Fischers. His wife, Kay; their daughter, Julie; all my other cousins—all of them are so kind and generous, and eager for me to go visit them.

With age and the extraordinary experiences I've had as a journalist and dognapper, I think I've picked up some wisdom and have finally uncrossed the wires, because now I see that I had forgotten to include myself among my possible sources of love. I no longer have to wait for it to show up. Now I see there are many sources of love, including the love that resides within me, and I draw happiness from all of it: wonderful friends, the beauty in nature, my lovely house, hikes in the mountains, my conversations with the Ohio Fischers, the writing of this story, the many dogs I've rescued, and, of course, Sammie and Ranger, such wise and loving cats.

When Sammie sits on my DSL modem and watches me work at the computer, the morning light streaming through the window onto her fur, bringing out its rich, auburn highlights, or when Ranger naps on my bed, or when my orchids come into bloom, I know moments of perfection. Such moments are everywhere, most of them brief flashes of something simple: a stranger's smile; a song on the radio calling up past loves; the December sun washing over my face; reading about some innocent prisoner who's been released; the sight of my neighbors, Seth and Tony, walking their dogs down the street.

Which brings me again to the subject of my neighbor Hank. I was going to tell you that the dog situation in my neighborhood is good now. The only incident requiring my intervention occurred last September, when I found a bewildered-looking schnauzer wandering in the middle of a busy street near my house. I managed to get him into my car and back to his grateful owner, who bought me two beautiful camellia bushes. Other than that incident, I remained, as always, ready to take action—legal or not—should the need arise. But I honestly thought I was done stealing dogs.

Then a month ago I made the mistake of walking down Hank's street. My heart sank as I saw his two dogs—Spot, the Dalmatian, and Husky, the shepherd, which he had adopted from the pound after I stole Sue—wandering in the street, without collars on, in terrible shape. I figured that Hank had learned his lesson from the disappearance of so many of his dogs and now took better care of them. But there they were, in the middle of the street, poking in the gutter for food. Spot was emaciated. Her ribs showed through her skin and she had a deep, bloody cut on her nose. Husky limped on his back leg and had some sort of skin disease. He scratched constantly, and most of the hair on his tail and backside was gone.

For the next week, I returned to the lookout post at my kitchen window and kept an eye on Hank's house. I would see him secure the wire gate with a piece of rope everyday when he left for work, which meant that along with everything else, his dogs were now confined in that small, junky side yard. Day after day I agonized over the suffering they must be going through.

One day when Hank was gone, I climbed over his fence, crossed his front yard, and undid the rope on the gate. Spot and Husky came bounding out, surprised but elated at their unexpected freedom. I let them run around in the street as I stood watch, wanting them to get some exercise at least. Another time when I saw Hank leave for work, my friend Brian, an animal lover and my new volunteer, helped me put Husky in the backseat of his truck and we took him to my vet.

"We need to keep him here to do some tests," Dr. Roth said. My mind raced with images of Hank returning home, finding that Husky was gone, and coming to look for me.

"Can you do it quickly?" I said. "I have a business appointment on the west side in a couple of hours."

"We'll do our best," he said.

An infected ingrown toenail was the reason for Husky's limp, and he didn't have mange, as I had thought. "He was loaded with fleas," said Dr. Roth, casting a disapproving look at me, the presumed owner. "You have to keep on top of fleas."

"Yes, Dr. Roth," I said. "I know. I will."

With treatment that I applied each day when Hank left his house, Husky's paw and skin began to heal and his hair grew back in. Still, I hadn't solved the main problem of the dogs' daily misery. *Do I really have to do this again?* I thought. *How will I find a home for two older dogs?* I sighed just thinking about the daunting prospect.

As the days passed, I kept seeing them in my mind, confined and lonely, behind Hank's gate. Then one morning I knew it was time, and all my apprehension vanished. I waited until I saw Hank's truck pull away, then put two leashes and some rawhide treats in my knapsack and left my house. Again I walked with purpose, my head held high, confidence filling every pore of my body. I climbed over his fence with ease, having done it so many times, and when I un-latched the gate, the dogs whimpered gratefully at my feet, perhaps sensing that this was the prison break they had longed for. I looked up and down the street, and when I saw no one was there, the dogs and I went quickly around the corner to a neighbor's house where they stayed, undercover, for four days.

We made up a flyer, posted it on the Internet, but no one responded. I called my friend Bonnie again, knowing she'd probably say no, but you just never knew. She did decline to help, but she thought her friend Kathleen might want a dog.

"I want to place them together," I said. "All they have is each other."

"That's going to be tough," she said, and it was. No one wanted two dogs. I boarded them at Wagville until I could find a home, and when the bill went over a thousand dollars, I hit my friends up for donations. Finally, after Christmas, a couple in Yosemite saw the flyer and contacted me. "I have a good feeling about your dogs," the woman said.

On the morning the dogs were leaving for Yosemite, I went to

Wagville to say good-bye. We huddled together for the last time, and then I helped them into my friend Brian's truck—he and his father had kindly offered to drive them to their new home, since I was writing frantically to meet a deadline.

As I pulled out of the driveway and headed home, I felt as I always did after I had rescued and placed a dog in a new home—great satisfaction tinged with melancholy, knowing I would probably never see them again. Turning onto San Fernando Road, I saw an old man dressed in shabby clothes shoo a pigeon off the bus bench, and it reminded me of an experience my mother told me about during one of her trips to visit Kate and me. I was seventeen years old then.

Mom said she had taken the Vine Street exit off the Hollywood Freeway as she usually did when she drove from Oxnard. She had stopped for the traffic light at the intersection of Vine and Franklin Avenue—jammed with cars as usual—when she saw a pigeon, looking startled and frightened, standing on the cement island between the lanes.

For a moment she hesitated, not wanting to block traffic, but then she put her car in park, turned off the engine, and got out. She walked to the center divider and gently approached the bird, "praying I wouldn't scare it off," she said.

By this time the light had turned green and horns were blaring. As she picked up the pigeon and walked across the lanes of stopped cars, the honking suddenly stopped. It was as if the drivers wanted to pay homage to her, perhaps recalling at that moment a finer part of themselves they had let slip away in life's frantic rush.

Mom walked slowly to the sidewalk. When she opened her hands, the pigeon fluttered its wings, trying to get its bearings, and then flew off into the sky.

ABOUT THE AUTHOR

Mary A. Fischer is a recipient of the John Bartlow Martin Award and has twice been a finalist for the National Magazine Award. For seven years, she was a senior writer at *GQ* and has contributed to *Men's Journal, New York* magazine, *Elle, Rolling Stone, Reader's Digest,* and *O Magazine*. In 2004 she was a consulting producer for ABC's Law and Justice Unit. She lives in Los Angeles.